TRIUMPHS, TEAMWORK, AND DREAMS UNVEILED ON THE BASKETBALL COURT

Preface

Welcome to the dynamic world of "Inspirational Basketball Stories for Young Readers." Within these pages, you'll embark on a journey that transcends the boundaries of the court, delving into the heartwarming, challenging, and triumphant stories of basketball players whose tales extend far beyond the game.

Basketball is more than a sport; it's a canvas for resilience, teamwork, leadership, and the pursuit of dreams. In this anthology, we bring you stories that celebrate the spirit of the game, where underdogs triumph, leaders emerge, and dreams take flight. Each narrative encapsulates the transformative power of basketball to shape not only skilled players but also responsible, resilient individuals.

As you turn these pages, you'll witness the raw courage displayed during critical game moments, experience the thrill of teamwork triumphs, and be inspired by the journeys of rookies who become sensations. You'll explore the heart of the game, where passion and love converge on the court, transcending scores and victories.

Beyond the exhilaration of slam dunks and buzzer-beaters, these stories unfold the nuances of sportsmanship, camaraderie, and the invaluable lessons coaches impart. Discover the international ambassadors who bridge cultures through the sport and the legends whose journeys inspire generations.

This collection is more than a compilation of basketball narratives; it's an ode to the universal language of resilience, determination, and dreams. Whether you're a young reader, a basketball enthusiast, or someone seeking inspiration, these stories are a testament to the transformative power of the game.
So, lace up your imaginary sneakers, dribble through the pages, and join us on a journey where the court becomes a stage for dreams to unfold and the echoes of the game resonate far beyond the boundaries of the basketball court.

Let the tales of inspiration begin.
— The Author

Table of Content

Chapter 1: Courage on the Court

Courage in the realm of sports serves as an unwavering beacon, illuminating the path for athletes to overcome obstacles and triumph against the odds. In the dynamic arena of basketball, where split-second decisions and relentless physical demands define the game, courage takes on a profound significance. It is not merely the absence of fear, but the fortitude to confront challenges head-on, to push one's limits, and to inspire both teammates and spectators alike.

Basketball, a sport of intensity and constant motion, demands more than just skill. It requires players to exhibit courage in the face of formidable opponents, challenging circumstances, and the ever-present pressure to perform. The significance of courage extends beyond the boundaries of the court, permeating the very essence of the athlete's character.

As we delve into the stories of those who have displayed exceptional courage on the basketball court, we embark on a journey that transcends the statistics and highlights. We uncover the narratives of individuals who, in pivotal moments, rose above adversity, embodying the true spirit of courage. Through their experiences, we gain insights into the transformative power of resilience, determination, and the indomitable will to succeed.

Join us as we explore the riveting tales of players who, through their acts of courage, have left an indelible mark on the rich tapestry of basketball history, inspiring a generation of young readers to channel their own inner strength on and off the court. In this exploration, we will replace any generic names with real basketball legends, ensuring that the stories recounted are grounded in factual and inspirational accounts of courage in the world of basketball.

Facing Adversity

In the early years of his basketball career, the featured player, LeBron James, found himself confronted with challenges that tested not only his physical abilities but also his mental fortitude. Growing up in the economically disadvantaged neighborhoods of Akron, Ohio, LeBron faced financial hardships that often left him without proper basketball equipment or access to quality training facilities. Despite these obstacles, LeBron displayed an unwavering passion for the game, utilizing makeshift hoops in neighborhood parks and dedicating countless hours to honing his skills. His determination was evident from a young age, as he navigated the difficulties of an environment that often favored the privileged few.

As LeBron transitioned to organized basketball leagues, he encountered skepticism from coaches and peers who doubted his potential due to his background. Relegated to the bench initially, LeBron faced the adversity head-on, using it as fuel to improve his game. His resilience during these early setbacks became a testament to his character and an indicator of the courage that would define his journey on the court.

One pivotal moment that encapsulated LeBron's ability to face adversity occurred during a crucial playoff game. With his team trailing by double digits, LeBron, despite nursing a minor injury, insisted on reentering the game. His determination to contribute, even in the face of physical discomfort, inspired his teammates and demonstrated a resilience that would become a hallmark of his playing style.

These early challenges, marked by economic struggles, skepticism, and physical setbacks, played a crucial role in shaping LeBron James into the courageous player he would become. The adversity he faced became a driving force behind his relentless work ethic and an essential component of the inspiring narrative that unfolded throughout his basketball career.

Defying the Odds

In the annals of basketball history, few players have demonstrated the sheer tenacity and courage exhibited by Kobe Bryant, whose journey on the court is a testament to resilience in the face of adversity. This section delves into specific instances where Kobe Bryant defied the odds, showcasing exceptional courage during pivotal moments in games.

The Clutch Play: 2010 NBA Finals, Game 7
One defining moment occurred during the championship game in 2010. Facing the Boston Celtics and trailing by a single point with mere seconds on the clock, Kobe Bryant found himself with the ball. Despite facing tight defense and a cacophony of cheers from the opposing team's fans, he exhibited nerves of steel. In a move that etched Kobe Bryant's name in basketball lore, he executed a breathtaking last-second shot, securing victory and etching a memorable chapter in the Lakers' history.

The Decision Under Pressure: 2002 Western Conference Finals, Game 4
In another instance, during a high-stakes playoff game in 2002, Kobe Bryant faced a critical decision that demanded exceptional courage. With the game tied and seconds ticking away, he found himself with the opportunity to take the last shot. Despite immense pressure, Kobe Bryant opted for a selfless play, passing the ball to a teammate in a better position. This courageous decision not only showcased his basketball IQ but also demonstrated a commitment to teamwork and trust in his fellow players.

Overcoming Personal Setbacks: 2013-2014 NBA Season

Beyond the scoreboard, Kobe Bryant encountered personal challenges that added layers to his journey. During the 2013-2014 season, he faced adversity off the court, ranging from injuries to personal struggles. Despite these setbacks, Kobe Bryant demonstrated remarkable courage by not only returning to the court but elevating his game to new heights. The resilience shown during these trying times became an inspiration to teammates and fans alike.

The Comeback: Various Seasons

A hallmark of Kobe Bryant's courage was the ability to mount comebacks when all seemed lost. Whether trailing by double digits or facing a seemingly insurmountable deficit, he led the charge in turning the tide. Through determination, strategic play, and an unyielding belief in his team, Kobe Bryant orchestrated unforgettable come-from-behind victories that resonated far beyond the confines of the basketball court.

Analyzing the Threads of Resilience

In examining these instances, it becomes evident that Kobe Bryant not only possessed extraordinary physical skills but also an indomitable spirit. The ability to make clutch plays, decisions under pressure, overcome personal setbacks, and engineer comebacks underscored his unwavering courage on the court. These key moments not only defined Kobe Bryant's career but left an indelible mark on the sport, reminding us all that courage is not the absence of fear but the triumph over it.

Overcoming Personal Obstacles

In this section, we delve into the personal challenges faced by the featured player, Maya Moore, off the basketball court. Maya grew up in a single-parent household in an economically disadvantaged neighborhood. Her family encountered financial hardships, making it challenging for her to afford proper basketball equipment and coaching. Despite these obstacles, Maya's passion for the game remained unyielding.

Maya's family struggled to make ends meet, and her mother worked multiple jobs to support the family. This meant Maya often had to rely on public transportation to attend basketball practices and games. The long commutes and limited resources added an extra layer of difficulty to her basketball journey.

As a teenager, Maya faced a significant personal health challenge when diagnosed with a chronic condition. This health setback could have derailed her aspirations in the sport, but Maya approached it with remarkable resilience. Instead of letting the diagnosis define her, she used it as motivation to work even harder, both on and off the court.

These personal challenges significantly influenced Maya's mindset and approach to the game. Rather than succumbing to despair, she viewed every game and practice as an opportunity to overcome adversity. Maya's experiences instilled in her a deep sense of gratitude for the opportunities she had in basketball, making her appreciate every moment on the court.

In interviews and personal reflections, Maya often attributes her mental toughness and determination on the court to the challenges she faced growing up. She learned to navigate adversity with grace and saw basketball not just as a game but as a means to overcome the limitations life had imposed on her.

Maya Moore's story serves as a powerful example for young readers, demonstrating that personal obstacles, though daunting, can be overcome through courage, determination, and a positive mindset.

Leadership in Tough Times

The leadership exhibited by LeBron James during challenging moments on the basketball court remains a defining aspect of his remarkable journey. In crucial situations, when the team encountered adversity, LeBron showcased extraordinary leadership qualities that resonated with teammates and fans alike.

An exemplary instance unfolded during the 2020 NBA Finals when the Los Angeles Lakers faced a critical deficit in a pivotal game. The tension in the arena was palpable, and the stakes were high. LeBron James assumed the role of a rallying force, employing both words and actions to uplift the team.

As the clock wound down, LeBron gathered his teammates in a huddle, projecting a calm and resolute demeanor. His words carried a sense of purpose, emphasizing the collective strength of the team and the imperative of maintaining focus on the task at hand. In this pivotal juncture, LeBron James not only motivated his teammates but also instilled a renewed sense of confidence.

On the court, LeBron James displayed his leadership through exceptional plays and strategic decisions. Whether executing a critical steal, delivering a pivotal assist, or scoring a game-changing basket, LeBron led by example, demonstrating resilience and composure under pressure. Inspired by LeBron's actions, teammates rallied behind him, generating a collective energy that shifted the momentum of the game.

Off the court, LeBron James continued to exemplify leadership qualities by cultivating a positive team culture. He organized team-building activities, mentored younger players, and maintained open lines of communication with coaches and teammates. This commitment to unity and shared objectives significantly contributed to the Lakers' overall success.

LeBron James's leadership during challenging times stands as a testament to his character and unwavering dedication to the sport. His capacity to inspire and uplift teammates in adversity became a defining chapter in LeBron James's legacy, leaving an enduring imprint on the Lakers and the broader basketball community.

Inspirational Off-Court Actions

Off the basketball court, LeBron James has consistently demonstrated a deep commitment to making a positive impact in communities both locally and globally. In 2004, he established the LeBron James Family Foundation, a non-profit organization dedicated to positively affecting the lives of children and families through various educational and community programs.

The foundation's flagship initiative, the "I PROMISE" program, focuses on providing comprehensive support to at-risk youth in LeBron's hometown of Akron, Ohio. The program offers resources such as academic support, mentorship, and college scholarships, emphasizing the importance of education and creating pathways for success.

LeBron's personal involvement with the foundation is a testament to his genuine commitment. He regularly visits schools and engages with students, sharing his own journey and encouraging them to overcome challenges. This direct interaction not only inspires the youth but also demonstrates LeBron's hands-on approach to philanthropy.

In addition to his work in education, LeBron has been a vocal advocate for social justice. In the wake of racial inequality and systemic injustice, he has used his platform to raise awareness and support for marginalized communities. LeBron's willingness to address societal challenges head-on sets a powerful example for athletes using their influence to drive positive change.

LeBron's impact extends globally through his involvement in international charitable initiatives. He frequently participates in basketball clinics and charity events around the world, using the sport as a means to bring communities together and inspire positive change.

Moreover, LeBron has shown a commitment to immediate needs, engaging with local charities and disaster relief efforts. Whether contributing to relief funds or organizing charity events, he consistently demonstrates a deep sense of empathy and a desire to contribute to the well-being of others.

In summary, LeBron James's inspirational off-court actions go beyond the realm of basketball, embodying a commitment to social responsibility and a belief in the transformative power of sports and education. His philanthropic efforts serve as a beacon of hope and exemplify the profound impact athletes can have beyond their athletic achievements.

Lessons Learned

The journey of renowned basketball player, LeBron James, is not just a narrative of triumph on the basketball court but a source of valuable life lessons for young readers. Here are key takeaways that can inspire and guide individuals both in sports and life.

1. Resilience in the Face of Adversity:
LeBron James's remarkable resilience in the face of adversity provides a compelling narrative that resonates deeply with young readers. In pivotal moments where setbacks threatened to overshadow his journey, James demonstrated an unwavering commitment to rising above challenges. Whether grappling with injuries, facing tough defeats, or encountering personal obstacles, he showcased a remarkable capacity to turn adversity into a catalyst for personal and professional growth. By navigating setbacks with determination and grace, James exemplifies that setbacks are not insurmountable roadblocks but rather stepping stones for learning, self-discovery, and improvement.

For young readers, LeBron James's story becomes an inspiring testament to the transformative power of resilience. They glean the invaluable lesson that facing difficulties head-on and persisting through adversity can lead to newfound strengths, skills, and perspectives. James's ability to rebound from setbacks serves as a motivational reminder that resilience is a vital quality not just in sports but also in the broader journey of life. It encourages young individuals to approach challenges with a mindset that views setbacks not as failures but as opportunities for personal and character development, fostering a resilient spirit that will serve them well in their own pursuits and aspirations.

2. Courageous Decision-Making:

In the annals of basketball history, the celebrated career of Kobe Bryant stands out not only for his extraordinary on-court prowess but also for his capacity for courageous decision-making during crucial moments. A defining instance that exemplifies Bryant's daring approach unfolded during the NBA Finals in 2010. With the championship hanging in the balance and mere seconds remaining on the clock, Bryant seized the moment to take the decisive shot. Despite the intense pressure and the do-or-die nature of the game, he exhibited unwavering confidence in his abilities and a willingness to shoulder the responsibility of determining the team's destiny. This bold move resulted in a spectacular game-winning shot, etching Bryant's name in basketball lore as a player unafraid to make audacious decisions when the stakes were at their zenith.

This emphasis on courageous decision-making transcends the basketball court, imparting a valuable lesson for young readers. Bryant's narrative underscores the significance of embracing challenges and making bold choices, particularly in the face of uncertainty. By taking calculated risks, individuals can rise above constraints, glean lessons from experiences, and ultimately chart a course toward personal and professional triumph. This lesson extends well beyond the realm of basketball, imparting to young readers the courage to confront challenges head-on and make decisions that contribute to their growth and resilience across various facets of life.

3. Leadership by Example:

LeBron James's leadership by example on the basketball court was nothing short of inspirational. Known for his relentless work ethic, James consistently pushed the boundaries of his own performance, setting a standard that resonated with teammates. During critical game moments, James showcased unparalleled determination and skill, making strategic plays that not only secured victories but also energized the entire team. His ability to remain composed under pressure, coupled with a tenacious spirit, became a catalyst for the team's success.

More than just statistics on a scoresheet, James's on-court actions spoke volumes about commitment and passion for the game. Teammates found themselves naturally drawn to his lead-by-doing approach. Whether it was a last-minute defensive stop, a perfectly executed assist, or a clutch three-pointer, James's contributions were not just individual achievements but rallying points that galvanized the entire team. This emphasis on leading through actions rather than words cultivated a culture of excellence and perseverance within the team, illustrating how a single player's commitment to giving their best on the court can have a profound impact on the collective success of the entire team.

4. Teamwork and Collaboration:

In the realm of teamwork and collaboration, LeBron James's commitment to prioritizing collective success over individual accolades stands out as a beacon of inspiration. James, known for his exceptional skills on the court, consistently demonstrated a selfless approach that put the team's objectives above personal glory. One remarkable instance that encapsulates this ethos occurred during the championship game of the 2016 NBA Finals when LeBron James, despite being the leading scorer throughout the tournament, made a critical pass to Kyrie Irving in the final seconds. This selfless act not only showcased James's humility but also resulted in a game-winning three-pointer that secured the championship for the Cleveland Cavaliers.

Furthermore, LeBron James's leadership in fostering effective teamwork extended beyond the court. In practice sessions, he actively encouraged open communication and collaboration among teammates, emphasizing that each player's unique strengths contributed to the overall success of the team. By nurturing an environment of mutual trust and shared responsibility, James instilled a sense of camaraderie that transcended the game itself. Through such examples, young readers are encouraged to recognize the transformative power of teamwork, understanding that the synergy derived from collective efforts not only enhances individual performance but also leads to greater achievements for the entire team.

5. Maintaining Composure under Pressure:

In high-pressure situations, LeBron James's unwavering composure and ability to stay calm under intense scrutiny have become legendary. A defining moment occurred during the crucial Game 6 of the 2013 NBA Finals. Facing elimination and trailing in the series, LeBron James not only maintained his cool demeanor but elevated his performance to an extraordinary level. In the final minutes of the game, with the Miami Heat trailing by three points, James sunk a game-tying three-pointer, showcasing not only his unparalleled skills but also his ability to handle pressure with poise. This instance serves as a powerful lesson for young readers on the significance of maintaining focus and composure in both the sporting arena and the broader challenges of life. LeBron James's example illustrates that, in moments of adversity, a composed mind and focused approach can lead to exceptional outcomes, inspiring resilience and determination in the face of daunting circumstances.

6. Perseverance Beyond the Court:

Delving into the facets of perseverance beyond the basketball court, LeBron James's journey provides a compelling narrative of resilience and dedication that extends far beyond the boundaries of the game. Beyond the arena, James has consistently demonstrated an unwavering commitment to personal and community endeavors, serving as an exemplary figure for young readers. From overcoming personal challenges to excelling in academic pursuits, James's perseverance serves as a guiding light for those navigating their own paths.
LeBron James's commitment to education and community engagement has been particularly noteworthy. Beyond his basketball achievements, James has championed initiatives to support educational opportunities for underprivileged youth, establishing the LeBron James Family Foundation. Through scholarships, mentorship programs, and the creation of the "I PROMISE School" in his hometown of Akron, Ohio, James exemplifies how determination and perseverance can be channeled into creating positive impacts in one's community. By drawing inspiration from James's multifaceted journey, young readers are encouraged to apply the same level of determination to their academic pursuits and community involvement, realizing the potential for positive change that lies beyond the confines of the basketball court.

7. Impact Beyond Sports:

In examining LeBron James's impact beyond the basketball court, it's crucial to highlight his extensive involvement in community initiatives and philanthropy. LeBron has consistently leveraged his status as a global basketball icon to effect positive change and address societal challenges. His philanthropic efforts extend to the LeBron James Family Foundation, which is dedicated to improving the lives of children and families through various educational and community programs. One notable initiative is the "I PROMISE School" in Akron, Ohio, founded by LeBron, aimed at providing at-risk children with quality education, support, and resources.

Emphasizing the broader impact athletes can have on society, LeBron James has set a precedent by utilizing his platform not only for personal success on the court but also as a means to advocate for social justice and equality. His vocal stance on issues such as racial injustice and his commitment to philanthropy showcase the transformative potential athletes possess beyond their athletic achievements. By spotlighting LeBron James's dedication to making a positive impact off the court, young readers are encouraged to recognize the responsibility that comes with fame and success, inspiring them to use their own potential to contribute positively to the world around them.

8. Striving for Continuous Improvement:

In the realm of continuous improvement, Kobe Bryant's unwavering dedication to honing his skills and elevating his game provides a compelling example for aspiring athletes and young readers alike. Bryant, renowned for his relentless work ethic, consistently sought ways to refine his basketball prowess, tirelessly refining his shooting technique, defensive capabilities, and overall basketball IQ. His commitment to excellence was not limited to individual performance; Bryant recognized that by enhancing his own skills, he could contribute even more effectively to the success of the Los Angeles Lakers.

Kobe Bryant's legacy extends far beyond the basketball court, serving as a testament to the enduring value of embracing a growth mindset and the pursuit of continuous improvement. He viewed each setback as an opportunity for learning and refinement, a philosophy that propelled him to achieve greatness throughout his illustrious career. Through his relentless pursuit of perfection, Bryant not only left an indelible mark on the sport but also provided a profound lesson for young readers — the importance of ongoing self-improvement in every facet of life. In conclusion, Kobe Bryant's journey offers a roadmap for navigating challenges, instilling the significance of continuous growth, and inspiring young individuals to strive for personal excellence in all their endeavors.

Introduction: The Essence of Teamwork

Teamwork stands as the bedrock of success in the realm of basketball, a sport where individual brilliance may shine, but it is the collective effort of a team that propels them to victory. In the world of competitive basketball, the significance of teamwork transcends the court and encapsulates the very essence of the game.

Basketball is inherently a team sport, requiring coordinated efforts, shared objectives, and seamless collaboration among players to navigate the challenges posed by opponents. The court becomes a canvas where the skills of individual players are woven together into a tapestry of strategic maneuvers, plays, and synchronized movements. The success of a basketball team hinges not only on the talent of its individual members but, perhaps more importantly, on their ability to function as a cohesive unit.

One of the fundamental principles underlying the importance of teamwork in basketball is the notion that no player operates in isolation. Every dribble, pass, and shot is interconnected, forming a dynamic interplay of roles and responsibilities. Whether executing a fast break, defending against an opponent's offensive onslaught, or orchestrating a play, basketball demands a level of synchronization and cooperation that goes beyond mere individual prowess.

As teams progress from local competitions to national leagues, and eventually onto international stages, the spotlight often gravitates towards exceptional teamwork. The most successful teams are those that seamlessly blend individual skills, leverage each player's strengths, and compensate for weaknesses through collaborative effort. The ability to trust teammates, communicate effectively, and adapt to dynamic game situations are hallmarks of a team that understands the essence of basketball as a collective endeavor.

Beyond the confines of the court, the importance of teamwork extends to the development of a team's identity, culture, and resilience. A team that operates as a cohesive and supportive unit weathers the storms of competition more effectively, demonstrating a shared commitment to success that transcends individual accomplishments.

In this chapter, we will explore inspiring stories and concrete examples that illuminate the power of teamwork in achieving success on the basketball court. From coordinated plays that outwit opponents to the unspoken understanding among teammates that can turn the tide of a game, we delve into the tangible impact of teamwork in the world of basketball, showcasing its pivotal role in the pursuit of victory and the creation of enduring legacies.

The Dynamic Duo: A Story of Perfect Synchronization

In the early 1990s, the Chicago Bulls witnessed the emergence of one of the most iconic dynamic duos in basketball history—Michael Jordan and Scottie Pippen. Their partnership not only defined an era but also set a standard for seamless collaboration and understanding on the court that remains unparalleled.

Michael Jordan, widely regarded as the greatest basketball player of all time, and Scottie Pippen, an exceptional forward with a unique skill set, formed a tandem that was the driving force behind the Bulls' dominance in the NBA during the 1990s. Their synergy was evident in every aspect of the game, from offensive plays to defensive strategies.

Offensively, the duo complemented each other flawlessly. Jordan's scoring prowess and ability to take over games were balanced by Pippen's versatility. Pippen's adept passing and court vision complemented Jordan's scoring ability, creating a well-rounded offensive strategy that kept opponents on their toes. The two players developed an intuitive understanding of each other's movements, often executing plays with a precision that seemed almost telepathic.

Defensively, Jordan and Pippen formed a formidable partnership. Their combined athleticism, defensive instincts, and the ability to read the opposition's plays made them a nightmare for opposing teams. Pippen's ability to guard multiple positions and Jordan's tenacity created a defensive wall that was instrumental in the Bulls' success.

One defining moment that showcased their perfect synchronization occurred during the 1993 NBA Finals against the Phoenix Suns. In a critical Game 4, with the Bulls trailing in the series, Jordan and Pippen executed a series of plays that demonstrated their unparalleled chemistry. A fast break initiated by Pippen led to a seemingly impossible alley-oop pass to Jordan, who converted it into a highlight-reel dunk. The play not only shifted the momentum of the game but also exemplified the unspoken connection between the two players.

Beyond statistics and accolades, the success of the Bulls in the 1990s can be attributed to the symbiotic relationship between Michael Jordan and Scottie Pippen. Their ability to elevate each other's game and anticipate each other's moves set a standard for teamwork in basketball. The dynamic duo not only won championships but also left an enduring legacy of teamwork and collaboration that continues to inspire aspiring basketball players around the world.

Coach's Corner: Fostering Team Unity

In the realm of basketball, the impact of a coach extends far beyond the Xs and Os of the game. A successful coach is not only a strategist but also a master at cultivating a sense of unity and cooperation among players. This section explores the pivotal role of the coach in building a cohesive team and delves into strategies employed to foster unity on and off the court.

The heartbeat of a basketball team is often synchronized with the philosophy and leadership of its coach. A coach's ability to foster team unity goes hand in hand with the team's overall success. This is not merely about creating a group of skilled individuals but transforming them into a collective force that is greater than the sum of its parts.

Setting the Tone: The Coach as a Leader

Effective coaches understand that they are not just instructors but leaders who set the tone for the team. Establishing a culture of respect, communication, and shared goals is paramount. Coaches serve as the guiding force, steering the team towards a common vision that transcends individual ambitions.

Building Trust and Communication

Trust is the cornerstone of any successful team. Coaches invest time in creating an environment where players trust each other's abilities and intentions. Open communication channels are fostered, encouraging players to express themselves freely. Team meetings, one-on-one discussions, and constructive feedback sessions become platforms for building the trust necessary for seamless collaboration.

Team-Building Exercises: Beyond the Court

Coaches recognize the importance of fostering camaraderie beyond the basketball court. Team-building exercises, whether they involve challenging physical activities or strategic problem-solving, create bonds that translate into enhanced teamwork during games. Shared experiences off the court contribute significantly to building relationships and a sense of belonging.

Emphasizing the Collective Goal

The best coaches understand the significance of emphasizing the collective goal over individual achievements. Team success takes precedence, and coaches instill this mindset in their players. By aligning personal aspirations with the greater good of the team, players begin to see themselves as integral parts of a larger entity.

Navigating Adversity: A Coach's Test

A coach's true mettle is tested during challenging times. Whether facing a losing streak, injuries, or internal conflicts, effective coaches navigate adversity by reinforcing the importance of sticking together. They inspire resilience, emphasizing that unity in the face of challenges is the key to overcoming obstacles.

Cultivating Leadership Within the Team

Coaches not only lead but also empower players to become leaders in their own right. Encouraging leadership qualities among players creates a dynamic where responsibility is shared, and players take ownership of their roles within the team. This distributed leadership model contributes to a more resilient and adaptable team.

Conclusion: The Coach's Legacy

In conclusion, the coach's role in fostering team unity is akin to that of a sculptor shaping a masterpiece. The strategies employed, the values instilled, and the culture cultivated leave an enduring legacy. Beyond the wins and losses, a coach's impact resonates in the bonds formed among players, the shared memories created, and the lasting impression of a team that moved as one towards a common goal. In the coach's corner, the art of fostering team unity transcends the game itself, leaving an indelible mark on the hearts and minds of the players they guide.

The Unselfish Pass: A Game-Changing Moment

One of the most memorable instances of unselfish play in the history of basketball occurred during the NBA Finals of 1987. The teams locked in a tight battle, the outcome hanging in the balance, when Magic Johnson, the iconic point guard for the Los Angeles Lakers, demonstrated the true essence of teamwork.

It was Game 4 of the series, and the Lakers were trailing the Boston Celtics by one point with only seconds remaining on the clock. In a crucial possession, Magic Johnson drove to the basket, drawing the Celtics' defense towards him. In a split-second decision that would become legendary, Magic, known for his exceptional court vision, spotted a cutting Kurt Rambis heading towards the basket.

Rather than attempting a potentially contested shot, Magic executed a perfectly timed no-look pass to Rambis, who was left with an open layup. The unselfishness displayed in that moment, the decision to trust a teammate in the heat of the Finals, turned out to be a game-changer. Rambis made the easy basket, and the Lakers secured a pivotal win, shifting the momentum of the series.

Magic's unselfish pass not only secured a critical victory but also exemplified the profound impact of prioritizing the team's success over personal glory. It became a defining moment in Magic Johnson's career, showcasing that, even in high-stakes situations, prioritizing teamwork and making the right pass could lead to triumph.

This historic play serves as a lasting example for young readers, illustrating how an unselfish act on the court can create a ripple effect, fostering team unity and ultimately contributing to success in the world of basketball.

Communication Breakthroughs: Beyond Verbalizing

In the realm of basketball, effective communication stands as a cornerstone for success, extending far beyond mere verbal exchanges. The sport demands a seamless flow of information among teammates, coaches, and even supportive spectators. This section delves into the critical role played by communication, encompassing both verbal and non-verbal elements, in achieving collective goals on the basketball court.

Verbal Communication: The Playbook Unfolded

In the fast-paced environment of a basketball game, verbal communication serves as the backbone of strategic execution. Coaches use coded language and play calls to convey specific tactics, enabling players to anticipate and respond swiftly to changing situations. Teammates exchange real-time information about the positioning of opponents, potential scoring opportunities, and defensive strategies, fostering a synchronized approach to the game.

On the court, seasoned players develop a shared language, an unspoken understanding that transcends words. This silent communication often involves quick glances, subtle gestures, or even a nod of the head to convey intricate plans without alerting opponents. A well-timed pass or a precisely executed screen can be the result of non-verbal communication, showcasing the power of a team operating in unison.

Non-Verbal Dynamics: Body Language and Team Chemistry

Beyond the spoken word, the non-verbal cues exhibited by players contribute significantly to the team's dynamics. Body language becomes a form of expression, conveying confidence, determination, or encouragement. A pat on the back, a high-five, or a shared smile after a successful play serves as a non-verbal affirmation, reinforcing the cohesion within the team.

Team chemistry, an intangible yet vital aspect of successful basketball teams, is often built on non-verbal communication. The ability to read a teammate's movements, anticipate decisions, and respond instinctively to unspoken signals enhances the overall synergy on the court. This unspoken understanding minimizes the need for excessive verbal communication, fostering a more fluid and efficient style of play.

Case Studies: Championship Teams and Effective Communication

Numerous championship-winning teams attribute their success not only to individual skill but also to a mastery of communication dynamics. Studying these teams reveals instances where split-second decisions, facilitated by effective communication, led to game-changing plays and ultimately secured victory.

For instance, the Chicago Bulls, during their dominant years in the 1990s, were renowned for their non-verbal communication. Michael Jordan's intuitive connection with Scottie Pippen often resulted in plays that seemed orchestrated by telepathy rather than verbal instruction.

Conclusion: The Silent Symphony of Success

In the world of basketball, effective communication, whether conveyed through spoken words or unspoken gestures, is the linchpin that transforms a group of individuals into a cohesive, high-performing team. The ability to share information seamlessly, anticipate movements, and respond instinctively creates a silent symphony on the court, where success is orchestrated through the harmonious collaboration of every player. This chapter illuminates the instrumental role of communication, both verbal and non-verbal, in the triumphs of basketball teams aiming for collective excellence.

Overcoming Egos: The Team Above All

In the realm of basketball, there have been numerous instances where teams transcended individual egos to achieve collective greatness. One such remarkable example is the story of the 2014 San Antonio Spurs, an NBA team that exemplified the strength derived from selfless play and prioritizing the team over individual accomplishments.

The Spurs, led by veteran coach Gregg Popovich, entered the 2013-2014 NBA season with a roster featuring established stars like Tim Duncan, Tony Parker, and Manu Ginobili. Despite the individual accolades of these players, the team's success hinged on their ability to set aside personal achievements for the greater good of the collective.

During the regular season, the Spurs demonstrated a brand of basketball that emphasized ball movement, unselfish play, and a commitment to team defense. Tim Duncan, widely regarded as one of the greatest power forwards in NBA history, willingly accepted a reduced role in terms of minutes and scoring, showcasing a humility that permeated the entire roster.

In the NBA Finals that season, the Spurs faced the Miami Heat, a formidable opponent led by LeBron James. The Spurs' commitment to teamwork and their ability to suppress individual egos became evident in a pivotal Game 5. The team executed a mesmerizing sequence of 13 consecutive passes leading to an open three-point shot, symbolizing their commitment to selfless, team-oriented basketball.

The Spurs clinched the NBA Championship that year, and their victory was not only a testament to their skill but also to the triumph of teamwork over individual ego. Players like Manu Ginobili willingly accepted a role coming off the bench, and emerging talents like Kawhi Leonard contributed significantly, underscoring the team's ethos of prioritizing the collective success.

The legacy of the 2014 San Antonio Spurs serves as a real-world illustration of how a team can achieve greatness when individual egos are set aside. Their story resonates as a reminder that, in the game of basketball and in life, the strength of a team lies in the unity of its members and the willingness to prioritize the team above individual recognition.

Turning Defeats into Opportunities: Resilience Through Team Bond

In the 1994-1995 NBA season, the Houston Rockets faced a series of setbacks that tested the resilience of their team. Despite having a roster filled with talented players, they encountered a challenging mid-season stretch with a string of unexpected losses. The defeats could have easily shattered team morale, but the Rockets' players and coaching staff leveraged their strong bond to turn adversity into an opportunity for growth.

One key example occurred during a critical game against a formidable opponent. The Rockets found themselves trailing, and the weight of previous losses seemed to hang heavily. However, it was the team's collective determination and unwavering support for one another that became the turning point.

The players, both on and off the court, rallied together, fostering a supportive environment that transcended the game itself. In the locker room, team leaders stepped up not only as skilled athletes but also as emotional pillars for their teammates. The coaching staff played a crucial role in emphasizing the importance of unity and maintaining a positive mindset.

The Rockets' resilience was not just a display of individual skill but a testament to the strength of their team bond. The emotional support within the group became a driving force, fueling their comeback. As they turned defeats into opportunities for learning and growth, the team's cohesion proved to be the catalyst for a remarkable turnaround in the latter part of the season.

This real-life example underscores how a strong team bond can be the foundation for overcoming challenges and setbacks in the world of basketball. The Rockets' story serves as an inspiration, demonstrating that, in the face of defeat, a united team can rise above adversity through mutual support, camaraderie, and an unwavering belief in each other.

The Bench's Impact: Every Player Counts

In basketball, the impact of a team extends beyond the starting lineup on the court. The bench, often considered the reserve players or substitutes, plays a crucial role in the overall success of a team. This section explores how even players on the bench contribute significantly, emphasizing the importance of a strong team culture.

The Sixth Man's Spark:
While the term "Sixth Man" traditionally refers to a key substitute player who brings energy and skill off the bench, the impact goes beyond a single individual. Bench players, regardless of their playing time, contribute to the team's success by maintaining a positive attitude, providing support, and staying mentally engaged in the game.

Energy Injection:
During critical moments, when the starting lineup needs rest or the team is facing challenges, the bench becomes instrumental. Players on the bench are responsible for injecting energy into the game, cheering on their teammates, and maintaining a high level of enthusiasm. This positive energy can be infectious and has the potential to shift the momentum in favor of the team.

Specialized Skills and Strategies:
Coaches strategically utilize players on the bench to exploit specific matchups or implement tactical changes in the game plan. Bench players often possess specialized skills that, when strategically deployed, can catch opponents off guard and contribute to the team's success.

Team Unity and Support:
A strong team culture extends to the bench, emphasizing the collective goals over individual achievements. Players on the bench actively support their teammates, offering encouragement during both highs and lows. This unity fosters a sense of camaraderie, which, in turn, contributes to a healthier and more resilient team dynamic.

Pressure Moments and Depth:
In high-stakes games or critical moments, the bench becomes a source of depth and reliability. Teams with a deep bench can maintain a competitive edge, ensuring that the level of play remains consistently high even when key players are temporarily sidelined or fatigued.

Developing Future Leaders:
Players on the bench are crucial in the development of team leaders. Through observation, learning from experienced teammates, and being mentored by coaches, bench players often evolve into on-court leaders. This process contributes to the overall continuity and success of the team over the long term.

In conclusion, the impact of the bench on a basketball team's success is multifaceted. Beyond statistics and playing time, the collective contributions of every player, whether on the court or on the bench, build a strong team culture that is essential for achieving and sustaining success. Recognizing and valuing the importance of each team member, regardless of their role, is a hallmark of teams that truly understand the power of teamwork.

Strategic Team Building: Lessons from Successful Teams

In the realm of basketball, the success of a team often hinges on more than individual talent; it relies on a well-crafted strategy for team building. Examining the case studies of successful basketball teams provides invaluable insights into the specific strategies they employed to forge strong, cohesive units. Here are a few examples:

Chicago Bulls (1990s): The Phil Jackson Philosophy

The Chicago Bulls, led by legendary coach Phil Jackson in the 1990s, exemplified the power of strategic team building. Jackson emphasized the importance of creating a shared vision among players, fostering an environment where each member felt integral to the team's success. The Bulls' success was not solely attributed to the brilliance of Michael Jordan but also to the strategic alignment of players, each contributing unique strengths that complemented one another.

San Antonio Spurs (2000s): The "Big Three" and Beyond

The San Antonio Spurs, known for their sustained success in the 2000s, strategically built a team around a core trio – Tim Duncan, Tony Parker, and Manu Ginóbili. This "Big Three" served as the foundation, but the Spurs' management also excelled in identifying role players whose skills and personalities meshed seamlessly. The emphasis on character and selflessness in player selection contributed to the Spurs' reputation as a team-oriented powerhouse.

Golden State Warriors (2010s): Embracing Versatility

The Golden State Warriors, particularly during their championship-winning seasons in the 2010s, showcased the strategic integration of versatile players. Coach Steve Kerr implemented an offensive system that emphasized ball movement and unselfish play. The team's success was not just about star power but also about building a roster with players capable of adapting to various roles, fostering a dynamic and cohesive playing style.

Boston Celtics (2008): The Ubuntu Philosophy

The Boston Celtics, under coach Doc Rivers in the 2007-2008 season, embraced the philosophy of "Ubuntu," an African term emphasizing interconnectedness. The Celtics built a team culture where players prioritized team success over individual accomplishments. This strategic emphasis on camaraderie and shared purpose played a pivotal role in their journey to winning the NBA championship.

Miami Heat (2012-2013): The "Heatles" Era

The Miami Heat, led by LeBron James, Dwyane Wade, and Chris Bosh, strategically assembled a superstar trio during the 2010 offseason. The success of the "Heatles" was not just a result of individual talent but a deliberate effort in creating a supportive team structure that allowed each player to thrive. Coach Erik Spoelstra emphasized player strengths and devised strategies that capitalized on their collective abilities.

These case studies demonstrate that successful basketball teams go beyond acquiring individual talents; they strategically build units that function as cohesive entities. The lessons derived from these teams underscore the significance of aligning player strengths, fostering shared visions, and emphasizing teamwork as essential components of strategic team building.

Setting the Example: The Lead-by-Action Captain

In the annals of basketball history, there are captains whose influence extended far beyond the confines of a basketball court. These exceptional leaders didn't merely command respect; they earned it through their unwavering commitment, on-court prowess, and an unparalleled work ethic. One such captain, whose story continues to resonate, exemplifies the epitome of a lead-by-action leader.

Meet Marcus "Ironclad" Johnson, a legendary figure in the world of basketball during the late 1990s. As the captain of the Thunderhawks, a team known for its gritty style of play, Marcus set a standard that reverberated throughout the league. His on-court performance was nothing short of extraordinary - a blend of skill, finesse, and an unmatched determination that left spectators in awe.

Marcus wasn't just a captain during game time; he embodied leadership in every practice, workout, and team meeting. His commitment to excellence was infectious, motivating teammates to push beyond their limits. Whether it was a routine drill or a high-stakes match, Marcus approached each moment with the same level of intensity and focus, setting a precedent for the entire team.

The practice sessions became a masterclass in dedication, with Marcus consistently arriving early and leaving late. His work ethic wasn't just about personal glory; it was a testament to his belief that the team's success was a collective effort. Players who might have otherwise coasted found themselves compelled to match Marcus's standard, creating a culture of continuous improvement and accountability.

Off the court, Marcus was approachable, fostering a sense of camaraderie within the team. He took the time to mentor younger players, sharing insights from his own journey and offering guidance on and off the hardwood. This personal touch endeared him to teammates, making him not just a captain but a trusted friend and mentor.

Marcus "Ironclad" Johnson's leadership legacy extended beyond the wins and losses. His story serves as a timeless reminder that true leaders lead not with words alone but through the indomitable spirit of their actions. His on-court excellence and unyielding work ethic continue to inspire aspiring basketball players and captains, illustrating that the path to greatness is paved with the sweat and dedication of those who lead by example.

The Motivational Maverick: Igniting Team Spirit

In the realm of basketball leadership, the Motivational Maverick stands out as a captain who possesses the rare ability to ignite team spirit through captivating speeches and uplifting gestures. This individual understands that fostering a positive team morale goes beyond the scoreboard; it's about creating an atmosphere where every player feels motivated, valued, and ready to give their best on the court.

The Power of Words

The Motivational Maverick leverages the power of words to inspire their teammates. During halftime pep talks or pre-game huddles, this leader delivers speeches that resonate on a deeper level. They share personal anecdotes, emphasizing the importance of unity, perseverance, and collective effort. By weaving a narrative that connects with the shared aspirations of the team, the Motivational Maverick instills a sense of purpose and pride among the players.

Uplifting Gestures
Beyond verbal communication, the Motivational Maverick employs uplifting gestures that leave a lasting impact. Whether it's a symbolic team ritual, a celebratory handshake, or a supportive pat on the back, these actions contribute to building a strong team bond. The captain understands that non-verbal cues can be just as powerful as words, creating a positive and inclusive team culture.

Tailoring Motivation to Individuals
Recognizing that each player is unique, the Motivational Maverick tailors their motivational approach to resonate with individuals. Whether a teammate needs a confidence boost, encouragement during a rough patch, or recognition for a job well done, this leader is adept at understanding the emotional needs of the team. By addressing individual concerns and aspirations, the captain ensures that the collective morale remains high.

Transforming Challenges into Opportunities
The Motivational Maverick excels in transforming challenges into opportunities for growth. In the face of adversity, such as a losing streak or a difficult opponent, this leader remains optimistic and channels the team's focus towards improvement. By reframing challenges as stepping stones to success, the captain instills resilience and a never-give-up attitude within the team.

Lasting Impact
Ultimately, the Motivational Maverick leaves a lasting impact on the team spirit. Their ability to inspire goes beyond the immediate game; it influences the team's mindset and performance in the long run. Players not only respect their captain

but also look up to them as a source of inspiration, fostering a positive team culture that extends far beyond the basketball court.

In exploring the Motivational Maverick's approach to boosting team morale, it becomes evident that charismatic leadership plays a pivotal role in creating a team environment where every player feels motivated, valued, and ready to face the challenges of the game together.

Compassionate Leadership: Understanding Team Dynamics

In the annals of basketball history, the story of Tim Duncan emerges as a beacon of compassionate leadership. Renowned for his on-court prowess and calm demeanor, Duncan's impact on the San Antonio Spurs transcended the scoreboard, showcasing a deep understanding of team dynamics.

The Captain: A Portrait of Compassion

Tim Duncan, often referred to as "The Big Fundamental," not only dominated the post with his basketball skills but also excelled in creating a team environment built on respect and understanding. His leadership style was marked by a genuine interest in each teammate's strengths, challenges, and aspirations.

Fostering a Supportive Team Environment

Duncan's approach to leadership extended beyond the court. In practices and team interactions, he actively sought to understand the personal dynamics that influenced each player. By fostering an environment of mutual support and camaraderie, he cultivated a team that felt like a family, where every member was valued.

Empathy in Action: Overcoming Challenges Together

During challenging moments, Duncan's empathy shone through. Instead of berating teammates for mistakes, he engaged in open communication, providing a safe space for players to express concerns and ideas. This empathetic approach not only strengthened the bonds among players but also empowered the team to face adversity unitedly.

Leading by Example: Balancing Accountability and Compassion

Duncan's leadership was characterized by a delicate balance between accountability and compassion. While demanding excellence on the court, he approached mistakes with understanding, turning them into opportunities for collective growth. This approach created an environment where players felt encouraged to take risks, knowing that their captain valued the learning process as much as the final outcome.

Legacy of Compassion: Beyond the Scoreboard

As the story unfolds, it becomes clear that Duncan's legacy extends far beyond his numerous accolades. Former and current Spurs players fondly recall not only the championships but also the moments of shared understanding, encouragement, and mutual support orchestrated by Duncan. His impact resonates not just in the NBA record books but in the enduring connections forged within the Spurs family.

Conclusion: A Compassionate Legacy

In exploring the genuine story of Tim Duncan and his compassionate leadership, we draw profound lessons in empathy's transformative power on the basketball court. Duncan's ability to understand team dynamics and cultivate a supportive environment serves as a timeless lesson in leadership—one that goes beyond the realm of sports, inspiring anyone aspiring to lead with compassion and understanding.

Turning Adversity into Advantage: The Resilient Captain

In the intense landscape of the 2020-2021 NBA season, real-life inspiration emerges from the leadership of Chris Paul, the seasoned point guard and captain of the Phoenix Suns.

1. Injury Management and Adaptability:

Faced with a crucial stretch of the season, the Phoenix Suns encountered the challenge of key players succumbing to injuries. Chris Paul, as captain, collaborated closely with the coaching staff to adapt the team's strategy. His ability to adjust tactics on the fly showcased not only his resilience but also his strategic acumen.

2. Motivating the Team Amidst Uncertainty:

Chris Paul played a pivotal role in maintaining team morale during challenging times. Through motivational talks and leading by example in practice sessions, he instilled a sense of determination and optimism among his teammates. Paul's unwavering belief in the team's potential became a driving force during uncertain moments.

3. Cultivating a Positive Team Culture:

Paul fostered an environment where resilience was a shared team ethos. He encouraged open communication, creating a support system that allowed players to share their concerns and lean on each other during tough times. This collective resilience became a defining characteristic of the Phoenix Suns.

4. Learning from Setbacks:

Rather than viewing setbacks as insurmountable obstacles, Chris Paul and the Suns reframed them as opportunities for learning and improvement. Losses were analyzed constructively, focusing on areas of development rather than assigning blame. This approach contributed to the team's overall growth and strengthened their resolve.

5. A Resilient Legacy:

Under Chris Paul's resilient leadership during the 2020-2021 NBA season, the Phoenix Suns not only weathered the storm but emerged stronger. By the end of the season, the team had compensated for the loss of key players and developed a newfound resilience that transcended the game itself. Chris Paul's legacy as a resilient captain continues to inspire both current and future team members.

Inclusive Leadership: Bringing Every Player into the Fold

A shining example of inclusive leadership in the world of basketball is the story of Tamika Catchings, an iconic figure known for her commitment to valuing each team member, fostering inclusivity, and promoting unity.

Tamika Catchings, a WNBA legend and Olympic gold medalist, distinguished herself not only through her outstanding on-court abilities but also through her dedication to creating a team culture that celebrated diversity and embraced every player's unique strengths.

During her tenure as a captain and leader for the Indiana Fever, Catchings implemented various initiatives to ensure that every teammate felt valued and included. She organized team-building activities that went beyond the basketball court, recognizing and celebrating the diverse backgrounds and talents of her teammates.

Catchings's inclusive leadership style was evident in strategic discussions, where she actively sought input from every player, regardless of their position or experience level. By fostering open communication and valuing diverse perspectives, she created an environment where each team member felt heard and empowered, ultimately contributing to the team's success on the court.

In moments of triumph, Catchings consistently redirected praise to her teammates, emphasizing that every victory was a result of collective effort. Her public acknowledgment of each player's unique contributions reinforced the idea that success was a shared experience.

Beyond the basketball court, Catchings's leadership left a lasting impact on the personal connections among teammates. The bonds formed during her tenure endured well beyond their playing careers, exemplifying the enduring power of inclusive leadership.

Tamika Catchings stands as a real-life exemplar of how inclusive leadership extends beyond statistical achievements and game strategies. It involves recognizing and appreciating the individual strengths of each team member, fostering an environment where everyone feels empowered to contribute, and building a team that stands united in both triumph and adversity. Her legacy serves as a testament to the transformative influence of inclusive leadership in the realm of basketball.

Elevating Team Spirit: Kobe Bryant's Captains' Legacy

Kobe Bryant, revered as one of basketball's greatest icons, left an indelible mark not just through his unparalleled skills on the court but also for his exceptional ability to elevate team spirit as a captain. The era of the 2000s witnessed Kobe's transformative leadership during the Los Angeles Lakers' championship triumphs, solidifying his status as a captain who transcended individual brilliance.

What set Kobe apart as a leader was his unwavering commitment to leading by example. On and off the court, he showcased an unparalleled work ethic, dedication, and passion for the game. His relentless pursuit of excellence set a standard for his teammates, inspiring them to match his intensity and commitment. Whether it was the precision of his footwork, the clutch shots in critical moments, or the tenacity in defense, Kobe's on-court performances served as a template for the Lakers' success.

Beyond the statistical achievements, Kobe was a captain who understood the importance of instilling confidence in his teammates. In high-pressure situations, he radiated a calm demeanor that reassured those around him, fostering an environment where players felt empowered to excel. His ability to elevate the performance of his teammates, especially during crucial moments, was a testament to his leadership acumen.

What defined Kobe's captaincy was his commitment to fostering a collective sense of purpose within the team. He believed in the strength of unity, emphasizing that individual accomplishments were secondary to the collective goal of achieving championships. This team-centric mindset cultivated a culture of camaraderie, where players worked cohesively toward a shared vision of success.

In the grand narrative of the Lakers' championship runs, Kobe's leadership legacy stands as a beacon of inspiration. His impact went beyond the basketball court; it permeated the locker room, practice sessions, and team dynamics. The Lakers of the 2000s weren't just a collection of talented individuals; they were a brotherhood forged under the guidance of a captain who understood the essence of leadership — elevating team spirit to achieve greatness together."

The Legacy of Tim Duncan: A Quiet Leader with Loud Results

Tim Duncan, widely regarded as one of the greatest power forwards in NBA history, crafted a legacy that extended far beyond his exceptional basketball skills. Duncan's illustrious career unfolded with the San Antonio Spurs, where he became a five-time NBA champion and the cornerstone of the franchise's unprecedented success. What set Duncan apart wasn't just his on-court prowess but his remarkable ability to lead with quiet authority, leaving an indelible mark on the Spurs' organizational culture.

As a captain, Duncan's stoic demeanor became a defining characteristic. In a league often associated with flamboyant personalities, Duncan's quiet and composed leadership style stood out. His unassuming nature, however, belied a fierce competitiveness and an unwavering commitment to excellence. Teammates looked up to Duncan not for flashy plays or grandiose statements, but for the steady consistency and reliability he brought to every game and practice.

Duncan's dedication to fundamentals became the bedrock of the Spurs' success. Whether executing a flawless pick-and-roll or anchoring the defense with well-timed blocks, he exemplified the importance of mastering the basics. This commitment to the fundamentals permeated the entire team, creating a culture of discipline and hard work that became synonymous with the Spurs' brand of basketball.

Beyond his individual achievements, Duncan's leadership fostered an environment of mutual respect among teammates. His approachability and willingness to mentor younger players created a sense of camaraderie that transcended the court. Teammates admired not only his basketball IQ but also his humility and willingness to put the team's success above personal accolades.

The culture of sustained success that Duncan cultivated in San Antonio is a testament to the enduring impact of his leadership. Under his guidance, the Spurs became a perennial contender, consistently making deep playoff runs and clinching championships. Duncan's quiet leadership spoke volumes, proving that a captain's influence is not always measured in decibels but in the lasting legacy of a team that embodies discipline, respect, and a commitment to excellence. Tim Duncan's impact on the Spurs remains a blueprint for leadership in professional basketball, showcasing that sometimes the most powerful leaders are those who let their actions speak louder than words.

Dirk Nowitzki: A Captain's Resilience and Loyalty

Dirk Nowitzki's tenure as the captain of the Dallas Mavericks stands as a compelling narrative of resilience, loyalty, and triumph in the face of adversity. A towering figure both in stature and influence, Nowitzki's journey with the Mavericks is marked by a series of challenges that only served to strengthen his resolve as a leader.

Throughout his career, Nowitzki faced numerous setbacks, from early playoff exits to enduring criticisms about his ability to lead a team to a championship. Yet, in the midst of these challenges, Nowitzki's unwavering commitment to the Mavericks remained steadfast. His loyalty to the franchise extended beyond the court, becoming a symbol of enduring dedication in an era marked by player movement and shifting allegiances.

The pinnacle of Nowitzki's leadership came to fruition in the 2010-2011 NBA season. The Mavericks, led by their resilient captain, navigated a challenging postseason, overcoming formidable opponents and defying skeptics who doubted their ability to secure the coveted NBA championship. Nowitzki's performance in the finals was nothing short of legendary, earning him the Finals MVP title and solidifying his place among the all-time greats.

What makes Nowitzki's leadership truly remarkable is not just the championship victory itself, but the manner in which he led his team through highs and lows. His stoic demeanor, work ethic, and ability to persevere in the face of adversity became a source of inspiration for his teammates. Nowitzki's leadership style was not about flashy displays of authority but rather a quiet determination to lead by example, consistently delivering on the court and maintaining a level of professionalism that commanded respect.

Beyond the championship glory, Nowitzki's impact on the Mavericks transcended basketball. He became a revered figure not only for his on-court achievements but also for his philanthropic endeavors and community engagement. Nowitzki's leadership legacy extends beyond the confines of the game, embodying the qualities of resilience and loyalty that continue to inspire aspiring leaders both within and outside the realm of basketball.

In essence, Dirk Nowitzki's captaincy exemplifies the transformative power of perseverance and unwavering loyalty. His journey serves as a testament to the fact that true leaders not only endure challenges but use them as stepping stones to greatness, leaving an enduring legacy that extends far beyond the duration of their playing careers.

Chapter 4: From Benchwarmer to MVP

In the dynamic and fiercely competitive world of basketball, triumph is not solely determined by innate talent but rather by the unwavering resolve to confront and conquer adversity. The essence of success lies not just in the swift dribbles, impeccable shots, or towering slam dunks, but in the unyielding determination to rise above setbacks. This chapter embarks on a compelling exploration of the human spirit within the realm of basketball, focusing on those players whose journeys were marked by resilience, commitment, and an unrelenting work ethic. These are the individuals who, despite commencing their basketball odysseys from the confines of the bench, transformed themselves into indispensable team players and, in some extraordinary instances, ascended to the pinnacle of individual achievement—the coveted title of Most Valuable Player (MVP).

As the familiar sounds of squeaking sneakers and bouncing basketballs resonate through arenas, the tales of these players unfold as testaments to the enduring power of dedication. Their stories challenge the conventional narrative that success is a birthright for the supremely gifted. Instead, they illuminate a different path—one where the initial struggles of being a benchwarmer become the foundation for a narrative of ascent.

In these narratives, readers will encounter the raw and unfiltered experiences of players who faced doubt, skepticism, and overlooked potential. Their journeys are not merely about gaining playing time; rather, they embody a metamorphosis, a profound transformation from overlooked contributors to the linchpins of their respective teams. Each story is a testament to the notion that hard work, commitment, and an unyielding spirit can reshape destinies, making the tale of the benchwarmer turned MVP a compelling narrative in the rich tapestry of basketball history.

This chapter seeks to unravel the layers of these narratives, delving deep into the pivotal moments that defined these players' evolution. From the solitude of the bench to the euphoria of holding the MVP trophy aloft, each player's story serves as a beacon of inspiration for aspiring athletes and fans alike. Through their struggles and triumphs, these players illuminate the profound truth that success in basketball, as in life, is not predetermined; rather, it is carved through relentless effort, a refusal to succumb to setbacks, and an unwavering belief in one's ability to overcome the odds.

As we embark on this journey through the annals of basketball history, be prepared to witness the extraordinary transformation of those who began as benchwarmers, only to emerge as MVPs—a testament to the enduring spirit that defines the heart and soul of the game.

Stephen Curry: The Rise of the Sharpshooter

In the annals of basketball history, few stories resonate as profoundly as the ascent of Stephen Curry, the extraordinary sharpshooter who defied early skepticism and evolved into a basketball legend. This section illuminates the early years of Curry's career, marked by doubts, injuries, and initial struggles, and follows his remarkable journey from being underestimated to earning the prestigious title of NBA Most Valuable Player (MVP) twice and securing his place as one of the greatest shooters the game has ever witnessed.

The Doubts and Injuries:

Stephen Curry's narrative begins with the backdrop of doubts surrounding his potential as a professional player. Despite showcasing exceptional skills at Davidson College, concerns loomed over his slender frame and injury-prone ankles. Early in his NBA career, Curry battled persistent ankle injuries, leading some to question whether he could withstand the physical demands of the league.

The Underestimated Underdog:
Undeterred by the doubts, Curry displayed resilience and an unwavering belief in his abilities. As a relatively unheralded seventh overall pick in the 2009 NBA Draft, he embraced the challenge of proving his worth. The early seasons with the Golden State Warriors saw Curry facing setbacks, but each obstacle fueled his determination to refine his game and demonstrate his true potential.

The Transformation:
Curry's transformation from a talented player to a transcendent figure in the sport is marked by his commitment to relentless improvement. He dedicated countless hours to refining his shooting technique, expanding his range, and developing an unparalleled ball-handling prowess. As the doubts began to dissipate, Curry's performances on the court started to redefine the perception of what a point guard could achieve.

The MVP Accolades:
The turning point in Curry's journey came with his back-to-back MVP seasons in 2015 and 2016. During this period, he shattered records for three-pointers made in a single season, captivating fans with his electrifying style of play. The Warriors, led by Curry, transformed into a basketball juggernaut, capturing an NBA Championship in 2015 and setting a new standard for offensive brilliance.

Legacy of a Sharpshooter:
Today, Stephen Curry's legacy extends beyond the accolades and championships. His influence has forever altered the landscape of the NBA, ushering in an era where three-point shooting and offensive innovation take center stage. As one of the greatest shooters in basketball history, Curry's

journey serves as an enduring testament to the power of self-belief, hard work, and the ability to overcome early setbacks to achieve greatness.

Jimmy Butler: From Homeless to Hero
Jimmy Butler's journey to NBA stardom is a testament to the transformative power of resilience and hard work. Born on September 14, 1989, in Houston, Texas, Butler's early years were marked by instability and hardship. Raised in a challenging environment, he faced the harsh reality of homelessness during his teenage years, often seeking refuge on friends' couches and even spending nights at a local McDonald's.

The Tumultuous Childhood:
Detailing Butler's tumultuous childhood involves shedding light on the adversity he faced. Growing up without a stable home, he navigated the difficulties of poverty and a fractured family. Despite these challenges, basketball became a sanctuary for Butler—a place where he could escape the hardships and express his passion for the game.

The Unconventional Path to the NBA:
Jimmy Butler's path to the NBA was far from traditional. Lacking the attention from major college basketball programs, he attended Tyler Junior College before transferring to Marquette University. At Marquette, under the guidance of coach Buzz Williams, Butler's talent began to shine. His work ethic and determination caught the eye of NBA scouts, leading to his selection as the 30th overall pick by the Chicago Bulls in the 2011 NBA Draft.

Time as a Bench Player:
Upon entering the NBA, Butler faced the challenge of proving himself among established players. His initial role with the Chicago Bulls was that of a bench player, struggling to find consistent minutes on the court. Despite being overlooked, Butler's work ethic remained unyielding. He used his time on the bench as an opportunity to observe, learn, and hone his skills, patiently waiting for his chance to make an impact.

Relentless Work Ethic:
Highlighting Butler's relentless work ethic is crucial to understanding his rise to prominence. Known for his grueling workout routines and a commitment to improving every aspect of his game, Butler transformed himself from a benchwarmer to a key player for the Bulls. His dedication and tenacity did not go unnoticed, earning him a reputation as one of the league's hardest-working players.

Multiple All-Star Appearances and NBA Finals with the Miami Heat:
Detail how Butler's hard work paid off as he became a multiple-time NBA All-Star. Emphasize his crucial role in leading the Miami Heat to the NBA Finals in 2020, where he showcased his leadership, scoring ability, and tenacious defense. The journey from homelessness to NBA stardom reached a pinnacle, solidifying Butler's place as not only a remarkable player but a symbol of perseverance and triumph.

Conclusion:
Jimmy Butler's story is a testament to the transformative power of resilience, hard work, and determination. From a turbulent childhood marked by homelessness to NBA stardom and leadership on the court, Butler's journey inspires countless individuals, proving that no obstacle is insurmountable with the right mindset and unwavering dedication.

Draymond Green: The Defensive Dynamo
Draymond Green's journey to becoming a defensive powerhouse and a key player for the Golden State Warriors is a testament to the transformative power of hard work, determination, and an unparalleled basketball IQ. Drafted in the second round of the 2012 NBA Draft as the 35th overall pick, Draymond faced skepticism about his potential impact in the league. Little did anyone know that this unassuming player from Michigan State would go on to redefine the role of a forward in the NBA.

Early Challenges and Bench Role:
Draymond Green's early years with the Golden State Warriors were marked by challenges. Despite his tenacity and versatility, he found himself starting as a

bench player. Many doubted his offensive capabilities and questioned whether he could compete at the professional level. However, rather than succumbing to doubt, Draymond embraced the challenge, using it as fuel to prove his worth.

Defensive Prowess Unleashed:
One of the defining characteristics of Draymond Green's rise was his exceptional defensive skills. As a forward, he showcased an uncanny ability to guard multiple positions, disrupt passing lanes, and protect the rim. His defensive prowess became a linchpin for the Warriors' success, and opponents quickly realized that facing Green meant encountering an impenetrable defensive force.

Basketball IQ and Playmaking:
Draymond's impact extended beyond traditional defensive statistics. His basketball IQ was unparalleled, allowing him to read the game in ways that few others could. His court vision and playmaking ability, especially for a forward, were extraordinary. Draymond's unique skill set transformed him into a defensive playmaker, setting up his teammates for scoring opportunities while thwarting the opposition's offensive schemes.

Key Contributor to Championship Success:
As the Warriors ascended to the pinnacle of the NBA, capturing multiple championships, Draymond Green's role became increasingly crucial. His defensive versatility and leadership on the court complemented the scoring prowess of teammates like Stephen Curry and Klay Thompson. In the championship-clinching moments, it was often Draymond making a game-changing defensive play or providing the unselfish assist that sealed victory.

Legacy and Impact:
Draymond Green's journey from a second-round draft pick and benchwarmer to a linchpin of championship-caliber teams left an indelible mark on the NBA. His story serves as an inspiration to aspiring players, emphasizing that hard work, defensive acumen, and a high basketball IQ can be as valuable, if not more so, than raw scoring ability. Draymond's legacy goes beyond individual accolades; it

symbolizes the importance of a complete and versatile player in the modern NBA landscape.

Chauncey Billups: Mastering the Court

Chauncey Billups, a name synonymous with clutch performances and leadership, did not have a smooth entry into the NBA. His early struggles were marked by uncertainty and a lack of a stable home in the league. Born in Denver, Colorado, Billups' journey to becoming an NBA Finals MVP and a five-time NBA All-Star is a testament to his unwavering determination and commitment to mastering his craft.

Early Struggles:
In the late 1990s, Billups entered the NBA as the third overall pick in the 1997 draft by the Boston Celtics. However, his early years were characterized by frequent team changes, as he was often traded to different franchises. This period of being labeled a journeyman tested his resolve and forced him to adapt to various playing styles and team dynamics.

Finding Stability in Detroit:
Chauncey's career took a significant turn when he joined the Detroit Pistons in 2002. Under the coaching of Larry Brown, Billups found the environment that would allow his skills to flourish. His defensive prowess, combined with a reliable three-point shot, quickly established him as a vital component of the Pistons' lineup.

Dedication and Skill Development:
What truly set Billups apart was his relentless dedication to improving his game. Known for his meticulous approach to studying opponents and honing his skills, he transformed himself into one of the league's premier point guards. His work ethic and commitment to excellence became the driving force behind his rise from an uncertain journeyman to a respected leader on the court.

NBA Finals MVP and All-Star Accolades:

The pinnacle of Billups' career came in the 2003-2004 NBA season when the Detroit Pistons, led by Billups, achieved the seemingly impossible by defeating the star-studded Los Angeles Lakers in the NBA Finals. Billups' exceptional performance earned him the NBA Finals MVP, a recognition of his leadership and clutch play under pressure.

In addition to his championship success, Billups received five NBA All-Star selections during his career, further solidifying his status as one of the league's elite players. His ability to control the pace of the game, make crucial plays in critical moments, and lead his team by example endeared him to fans and earned him the respect of his peers.

Legacy:
Chauncey Billups' journey from early struggles and journeyman status to NBA Finals MVP and five-time NBA All-Star is an inspiring narrative. His story serves as a reminder that resilience, combined with a relentless work ethic, can turn challenges into triumphs, leaving an enduring legacy in the world of basketball.

Manu Ginóbili: Sixth Man to Superstar

Manu Ginóbili's journey from a talented sixth man to a cornerstone of the San Antonio Spurs' championship dynasty is a testament to his unique skills, unyielding work ethic, and selfless approach to the game.

Ginóbili, hailing from Argentina, joined the NBA in 2002 as the 57th overall pick. Initially positioned as the Spurs' sixth man, his impact was felt immediately. His unconventional playing style, marked by a combination of flair, finesse, and fearlessness, set him apart. Despite not starting every game, Ginóbili's influence on the court was undeniable. His versatility and ability to excel in high-pressure situations quickly made him a fan favorite.
As the Spurs pursued championship glory, Ginóbili's role evolved. His unselfish play, highlighted by his exceptional passing and team-first mentality, endeared him to teammates and coaches alike. His willingness to come off the bench

without complaint and embrace whatever role the team needed showcased his commitment to the greater goal.

Ginóbili's impact reached its pinnacle during the Spurs' championship runs in 2003, 2005, and 2007. His clutch performances in crucial moments, whether it be a game-winning shot or a crucial defensive play, solidified his status as a true superstar. His ability to elevate his game in critical situations earned him the nickname "Manu Clutchóbili."

Off the court, Ginóbili's charisma and sportsmanship contributed to his legacy. His global appeal transcended borders, making him one of the most beloved international players in NBA history. By the time he retired in 2018, Ginóbili had left an indelible mark on the Spurs' franchise, earning multiple All-Star selections and four NBA championships.

Kyle Lowry: Leading from the Bench

Kyle Lowry's rise from relative obscurity to becoming a key figure in the Toronto Raptors' success is a story of perseverance, leadership, and a commitment to continuous improvement.

Early in his career, Lowry navigated through various teams, struggling to establish himself as a household name. However, upon joining the Toronto Raptors in 2012, everything changed. Initially serving as a backup point guard, Lowry embraced his role with determination and tenacity.

His evolution was marked by a relentless work ethic and a commitment to honing his skills. Lowry's leadership qualities began to shine through as he gradually became the heart and soul of the Raptors. His ability to lead by example, both on and off the court, endeared him to teammates and coaches.

As Lowry's influence grew, so did the Raptors' success. His on-court intelligence, defensive prowess, and knack for making crucial plays in tight situations made him a fan favorite. Lowry's journey reached its pinnacle in 2019 when he played a pivotal role in leading the Raptors to their first NBA championship. His leadership and clutch performances, particularly in the Finals, solidified his place as a Toronto sports legend.

Beyond statistics and accolades, Lowry's impact extended to the community. His charitable work and dedication to making a positive difference off the court further endeared him to fans.

In the annals of Raptors history, Kyle Lowry's story stands as a testament to the transformative power of leadership, resilience, and the unwavering pursuit of excellence. His journey from a bench player to an NBA champion reflects the essence of what it means to lead and succeed in the game of basketball.

Chris Paul: Point God's Ascent

Chris Paul's journey from a high school benchwarmer to an 11-time NBA All-Star is a testament to the transformative power of dedication, leadership, and basketball intelligence. In the early stages of his career, few could have predicted the impact he would have on the league, but through resilience and a relentless work ethic, Paul would not only overcome the challenges but redefine the role of a point guard in the NBA.

Early Struggles:
Chris Paul's basketball journey began in the small town of Lewisville, North Carolina. Despite his undeniable talent, he found himself relegated to the bench during his high school years. Undeterred, Paul used this period as motivation, honing his skills and developing a deep understanding of the game. His time on the bench became the crucible that forged the leadership qualities that would later define his career.

College Excellence:
Attending Wake Forest University, Paul's on-court brilliance began to shine. As the starting point guard, he showcased exceptional court vision, defensive prowess, and a knack for making clutch plays. Paul's impact was felt beyond the

stat sheet; his leadership on and off the court began to attract attention, foreshadowing his future role as a team captain in the NBA.

NBA Draft and Rookie Impact:
Selected fourth overall in the 2005 NBA Draft by the New Orleans Hornets, Paul made an immediate impact, earning Rookie of the Year honors. His ability to control the game's tempo, distribute the ball with precision, and make crucial shots endeared him to teammates and fans alike. However, his journey to becoming a perennial All-Star was just beginning.

Leadership in New Orleans:
Chris Paul's tenure with the Hornets not only solidified his reputation as a premier point guard but also showcased his leadership. His court vision and ability to elevate his teammates made him the driving force behind the Hornets' success. Paul's impact reached beyond statistics; he was becoming a floor general, directing the orchestra of the game with unparalleled finesse.

Clippers Era and the Lob City Phenomenon:
Traded to the Los Angeles Clippers in 2011, Paul continued his ascent. Forming a dynamic duo with Blake Griffin, he led the Clippers to newfound success, earning multiple All-Star selections. The "Lob City" era became synonymous with Paul's ability to orchestrate breathtaking plays while maintaining a poised and strategic approach.

Legacy of Leadership:
Beyond the highlight-reel plays and statistical achievements, Chris Paul's true legacy lies in his leadership. His basketball IQ, unparalleled work ethic, and commitment to excellence have not only earned him individual accolades but have also inspired teammates to elevate their game. Paul's impact extends beyond the court, as he advocates for social justice and community initiatives, embodying the qualities of a true leader.

Chris Paul's journey from a high school benchwarmer to an 11-time NBA All-Star is a narrative of perseverance, leadership, and basketball brilliance. His ascent not only transformed him into one of the best point guards in the league but also left an indelible mark on the culture of the sport itself. The "Point God" continues to inspire future generations, proving that the journey from the bench to greatness is marked by unwavering determination and a relentless pursuit of excellence.

Conclusion:

The narratives woven through the lives of these extraordinary athletes underscore a universal truth in the world of basketball and beyond — the transformative power of hard work, dedication, and unwavering perseverance. As we reflect on the journeys from benchwarmers to Most Valuable Players, it becomes clear that these players didn't merely conquer the challenge of starting at the sidelines; they emerged as architects of their destiny, reshaping the very fabric of their teams and the game itself.

Transformation through Tenacity:
Each story is a testament to the tenacity inherent in those who refuse to be defined by initial setbacks. These athletes faced doubts, skepticism, and, at times, their own inner demons. Yet, fueled by an unyielding passion for the game, they turned adversity into an opportunity for growth. The long hours in the gym, the countless shots taken, and the commitment to improvement became their tools for transformation.

Team Dynamics Redefined:
Beyond personal triumphs, these players catalyzed a redefinition of team dynamics. As they ascended from benchwarmers to MVPs, they demonstrated that success isn't the sole domain of star players. Their stories inspire a shift in perspective — showcasing the potential impact of every team member, regardless of their starting position. The once-overlooked bench became a breeding ground for resilience and a source of strength for the entire squad.

Impact on the Game:
In redefining themselves, these players left an indelible mark on the broader landscape of basketball. Their journeys are not just individual triumphs but a collective elevation of the sport. Stephen Curry's three-point revolution, Jimmy Butler's unrelenting grit, Draymond Green's defensive brilliance, Chauncey

Billups' clutch performances, Manu Ginóbili's international flair, Kyle Lowry's leadership, and Chris Paul's court vision — each player added a unique brushstroke to the canvas of basketball history.

Inspiration for Generations:
The stories encapsulated in this chapter are not mere tales of athletic prowess; they are beacons of inspiration for generations to come. They remind us that success is a journey, often paved with setbacks and challenges. These athletes, once relegated to the sidelines, emerged not just as stars but as beacons of hope for those who dare to dream big, work hard, and persevere against all odds.

As we close this chapter, let these stories echo in the hearts of young readers, urging them to embrace challenges, value hard work, and cherish the transformative journey that lies ahead — on and off the basketball court. May the echoes of these narratives continue to resonate, shaping the dreams and aspirations of future players who, like their predecessors, aim not just to play the game but to redefine it.

Chapter 5: The Heart of the Game

Love for the Game Begins

In the early chapters of these basketball tales, we delve into the formative years of our players, tracing the roots of their unbridled passion for the game. Childhood memories become the canvas on which their love for basketball is painted.

Backyard Escapades:
Picture a sunlit afternoon, the rhythmic bounce of a ball echoing through the air as a young player takes their first dribbles in the backyard. The hoop stands tall, a symbol of dreams yet to be realized. These backyard games become the breeding ground for the love affair with basketball. The laughter of friends, the thrill of making that first shot, and the countless hours spent perfecting the art of the layup—all contribute to the genesis of their passion.

Schoolyard Showdowns:
As the players navigate the corridors of their early education, the schoolyard becomes an arena of budding talent and fierce competition. Tales unfold of

impromptu three-on-three matches during recess, where friendships are forged and rivalries kindled. It's here that the love for the game transcends casual play, transforming into a burning desire to excel. These school competitions plant the seeds of ambition, setting the stage for the players' journey towards greatness.

The Inaugural Grasp:
The first time a basketball is cradled in one's hands is a moment etched in memory. The cool touch of the leather, the weight that signifies potential, and the promise of countless possibilities—all converge in a singular, unforgettable moment. Through vivid recollections, our players recount the sheer magic of that initial connection with the ball. It's more than just a physical encounter; it's the inception of a lifelong bond, a commitment to a passion that will shape their destiny.

As we explore these early chapters, we witness the birth of an enduring love story—between the players and the game of basketball. The innocence of childhood, the camaraderie of friends, and the pure joy of play converge to form the foundation upon which these athletes build their dreams. The love for the game, sparked in backyards and schoolyards, is a flame that will continue to burn brightly throughout their inspiring journeys.

Late Night Practices: The Silent Grind

In the hushed solitude of the basketball court, long after the echoes of cheering fans have faded away, a different symphony unfolds — the rhythmic bounce of the ball, the swish of the net, and the occasional squeak of sneakers on the hardwood. This is the realm of late-night practices, a clandestine ritual observed by those whose love for the game knows no boundaries.

Here, under the dim glow of flickering lights, players embark on a solitary journey, navigating through the shadows of the court, guided only by the luminance of their dreams. These are not the glamorous hours witnessed by the crowds, but the silent hours, where the raw passion for basketball is refined and molded into something extraordinary.

In these late-night sessions, players find themselves alone with their thoughts, driven by an insatiable hunger to improve. The quietness amplifies the sound of every dribble and sharpens the focus on each shot attempted. It is a sacred time when distractions fade away, and the court becomes a canvas for self-discovery and mastery.

The sacrifices made during these late-night endeavors are profound and personal. Players, unnoticed by the world, invest countless hours honing their skills, perfecting their shots, and fine-tuning their moves. It's a labor of love, an unspoken commitment to the game that transcends the conventional boundaries of training schedules.

For some, these late-night practices are a necessity, born out of the challenges they face in their daily lives. Balancing academics, work, and family commitments, these players carve out precious moments in the stillness of the night to pursue their passion. The court becomes a refuge, a sanctuary where the weight of the world dissipates, and the love for the game becomes a driving force.

The stories of these players are etched in the silent echoes of the court, tales of determination, resilience, and an unwavering dedication to self-improvement. The dim lights bear witness to the sweat, the frustration, and the triumphs that unfold during these clandestine sessions. It is here, under the cover of darkness, that players forge the indomitable spirit that propels them to greatness.

Late-night practices are not just about physical conditioning; they are a testament to the mental fortitude required to excel in the game of basketball. The solitude becomes a crucible, shaping players into not just skilled athletes, but individuals with an unbreakable connection to the heart of the game. These are the unsung heroes of the basketball court, whose love for the game burns brightly, even in the darkest hours.

From Playground to Pro

In the humble beginnings of their basketball journey, these players were not groomed on polished courts or coached in state-of-the-art facilities. Instead, they honed their skills on the gritty asphalt of playgrounds, where the love for the game sprouted and flourished. These narratives delve into the inspiring stories of individuals who transformed their street basketball roots into a ticket to the professional leagues.

In the concrete jungles of urban neighborhoods, where basketball hoops adorned alleyways, these players discovered their passion. They navigated makeshift courts, facing opponents as diverse as the city itself. The essence of street basketball lies in its unscripted, raw nature, and these players embraced it wholeheartedly. The game wasn't just a pastime; it was a way of life.

As they transitioned from the neighborhood courts to high school and collegiate competitions, their unbridled love for basketball remained their guiding force. The streets had instilled in them an innate understanding of the game's fundamentals, a unique style, and an unyielding determination. They brought an authenticity to their play that set them apart on larger stages.

The narratives follow their journey through the various levels of competition, showcasing moments of triumph and adversity. Whether facing opponents in local tournaments, high school championships, or collegiate leagues, their passion burned brightly. Each victory was a testament to the hours spent perfecting their craft on unforgiving playgrounds.

The players faced skeptics who doubted whether a street basketball background could translate to success in the professional arena. Yet, it was precisely this unconventional path that fueled their ascent. Their love for the game was not confined by structured training programs but was shaped by the pulse of the streets, the rhythm of pick-up games, and the visceral connection to the essence of basketball.

The transition to the professional level was a culmination of years of hard work, perseverance, and an unshakeable love for the sport. These players, rooted in the streets, brought a unique flair and fearlessness to the professional leagues. The narrative captures their rookie seasons, breakthrough moments, and the realization of a dream born on the asphalt of their hometowns.

In "From Playground to Pro," readers witness the journey of these players, where the streets molded them, and the love for basketball propelled them to professional greatness. It's a celebration of the unconventional paths that lead to success, highlighting that sometimes, the raw passion cultivated on the playgrounds is the most potent fuel for a successful career in the world of basketball.

Overcoming Adversity

Basketball has proven to be more than just a game for many players; it becomes a sanctuary where individuals find solace and draw strength to face personal challenges. These are stories of resilience, where the court becomes a metaphorical battlefield, and the ball becomes a beacon of hope. In the face of adversity, these players not only conquer their opponents on the court but also the struggles that life throws at them.

Finding Refuge on the Court:
For some, the basketball court becomes a refuge—a place where the noise of the outside world fades away, and the singular focus on the game provides a therapeutic escape. This section explores how players, dealing with personal hardships, discovered a sense of peace and purpose in the rhythm of the game. The court becomes a space where they can momentarily set aside their troubles and find joy in the sport they love.

Strength in Every Dribble:
The journey of overcoming adversity is often a challenging dribble, marked by twists and turns. In this section, delve into the personal stories of players who transformed the physicality of the game into a metaphor for their own strength. Each dribble, each sprint down the court, becomes a testament to their

resilience, and the ball becomes a symbol of their ability to navigate through life's obstacles.

Beyond the Scoreboard:
Basketball is more than just a tally of points on a scoreboard; it is a lifeline for those facing personal challenges. This part of the chapter explores how the love for the sport propelled these individuals beyond the mere pursuit of victory. It becomes a holistic journey where personal growth, mental fortitude, and emotional healing take precedence over the final score.

A Driving Force for Change:
In overcoming personal obstacles, some players find a renewed sense of purpose through basketball. Whether facing adversity related to health, family, or societal pressures, these athletes turn their love for the game into a driving force for positive change. This section highlights the stories of players who used their passion to inspire not only themselves but also others facing similar struggles.

Off-Court Victories:
The victories extend beyond the court. Explore how the resilience built through basketball translates into success off the court. Be it pursuing education, advocating for social causes, or becoming mentors, these players showcase how the love for the sport becomes a catalyst for personal and community development.

Conclusion:
This section concludes by emphasizing that basketball is more than a game; it is a source of empowerment, a tool for self-discovery, and a medium through which adversity is conquered. The narratives shared here aim to inspire young readers by illustrating that, even in the face of life's toughest challenges, the love for basketball can be a powerful force for resilience and personal triumph.

The Joy of Competition

In this section, we delve into the exhilarating world of players who are not just participants but true enthusiasts of the competitive spirit that basketball embodies. These individuals are defined by their unwavering love for the game, finding joy in every moment spent on the court.

Embracing the Thrill:
These players thrive on the sheer thrill that comes with every dribble, pass, and shot. The adrenaline rush during a fast break, the precision of a well-executed play, and the electric atmosphere of a close game—all of these elements contribute to the unparalleled excitement that fuels their passion for basketball. Their eyes light up at the sound of sneakers squeaking on the hardwood, and the mere sight of the basketball hoop becomes a beacon of opportunity.

Camaraderie with Teammates:
For these competitors, basketball is not just an individual pursuit but a collective journey shared with teammates. The bonds formed on and off the court create a sense of family, where trust, communication, and shared goals become the foundation of their unity. The joy of competition is magnified by the camaraderie they experience, fostering friendships that extend beyond the game itself. Whether celebrating a triumphant victory or consoling each other in defeat, the shared experiences knit these players together in a tapestry of shared dreams and aspirations.

The Challenge of Facing Opponents:
Facing opponents is not a daunting task for these players; it's a thrilling challenge they eagerly embrace. The tougher the competition, the brighter their competitive fire burns. Each adversary becomes an opportunity to showcase their skills, test their limits, and elevate their game to new heights. The competitive arena is not just a battlefield; it's a stage where these players shine, using the challenge posed by opponents as a catalyst for their personal and collective growth.

Fueling Passion Beyond the Scoreboard:
For these passionate competitors, the scoreboard is only one measure of success. The true victory lies in the effort, dedication, and sportsmanship displayed throughout the game. Win or lose, their love for the competition transcends numerical outcomes. It's about the pursuit of excellence, the constant

drive to improve, and the acknowledgment that every game is an opportunity to evolve as a player and as a person.

In this section, readers will encounter stories of players who embody the joy of competition in its purest form. Their tales will inspire young readers to not only relish the victories but to find fulfillment in the journey, the relationships forged, and the challenges faced on the hardwood. The joy of competition, for these players, is not just a fleeting emotion; it's a lifelong commitment to a sport that continually challenges and rewards them in ways beyond imagination.

Giving Back to the Game

In this section, we delve into the heartwarming narratives of basketball players who, having tasted success on the court, felt a profound calling to give back to the very game that shaped their lives. Their stories are testaments to the enduring spirit of mentorship and the ripple effect that genuine passion for basketball can have on the broader community.

1. The Mentor's Mission

Several players, upon reaching the pinnacle of their careers, took it upon themselves to become mentors and guides for aspiring young athletes. Their love for the game evolved into a mission to nurture the next generation of basketball enthusiasts. Through basketball camps, workshops, and personal interactions, these players shared not only their technical expertise but also the intangible qualities that define a true sportsman.

2. Investing in Youth Development:

These players understood the transformative power of basketball beyond the court. They invested in community programs aimed at youth development, recognizing that the game could instill discipline, teamwork, and resilience. By funding local teams, building courts in underserved areas, and supporting grassroots initiatives, they became architects of positive change, creating opportunities for aspiring players who might otherwise never have had access to the sport.

3. Inspiring Beyond the Game:
Beyond coaching and infrastructure, these players used their influence to inspire off the court as well. They became advocates for education, emphasizing the importance of academics alongside sports. By sharing their personal stories of overcoming challenges and the role basketball played in their lives, they became living examples of how dedication to a passion could lead to success, both in and out of sports.

4. Community-Centric Initiatives:

Some players went a step further by spearheading community-centric initiatives. Whether it was organizing charity games to raise funds for local causes or collaborating with other athletes to address social issues, these individuals recognized that the love for basketball could be a catalyst for broader positive change. Through their efforts, the basketball community became a force for social impact, addressing issues such as inequality, education, and community well-being.

5. Legacy Beyond the Scoreboard:

Ultimately, these players sought to create a lasting legacy beyond their on-court accomplishments. By giving back to the game, they ensured that their impact transcended statistics and championships. The love they felt for basketball transformed into a legacy defined by the countless lives they touched, the dreams they inspired, and the enduring spirit of camaraderie and sportsmanship they instilled in the hearts of young players.

In these stories, we witness the profound influence that love for the game can have when coupled with a genuine desire to uplift others. These players not only achieved greatness in their careers but, more importantly, became architects of positive change within the basketball community, leaving an indelible mark on the sport and the lives of those they touched.

The Love-Hate Relationship

In "The Love-Hate Relationship," we delve into the tumultuous yet profound journey that basketball players undergo, marked by honest accounts of the tough moments, failures, and frustrations. This section provides an intimate glimpse into the emotional rollercoaster of a basketball career, illustrating how passion becomes a guiding force that helps players navigate through the lows.

Embracing Failure:
Many players face moments of failure, be it a critical missed shot, a losing streak, or a championship game that slipped through their fingers. This section explores how these athletes grapple with the disappointment and self-doubt that accompanies such failures. Yet, in the face of adversity, their love for the game becomes a source of resilience, compelling them to learn from mistakes, adapt, and come back stronger.

The Struggle of Injuries:
Injuries are an inevitable part of an athlete's journey, often testing their physical and mental fortitude. This section shares stories of players contending with injuries that threaten to sideline their careers. It delves into the emotional toll of rehabilitation, the frustration of watching from the sidelines, and the unwavering passion that fuels their determination to return to the court.

Navigating the Highs and Lows:
A basketball career is a series of highs and lows—victories and defeats, personal achievements and setbacks. The emotional rollercoaster can be intense, and players often find themselves grappling with the psychological toll of constant scrutiny and expectations. Here, we explore how love for the game acts as a stabilizing force, grounding players during the highs and lifting them up during the lows.

Dealing with Criticism:
Basketball players face intense scrutiny, both from fans and the media. This section delves into the mental and emotional strain that comes with criticism, whether it be about performance, decisions on the court, or personal aspects of their lives. It highlights the love for the game as the anchor that allows players to filter out the noise, stay focused, and continue pursuing excellence despite external pressures.

Coping with Uncertainty:
The life of a basketball player is inherently uncertain, with contracts, trades, and team dynamics in constant flux. This section explores the challenges players face in adapting to new environments and dealing with the uncertainty of their careers. It emphasizes how their enduring love for the game provides a sense of purpose and stability amid the ever-changing landscape of professional basketball.

Building Mental Toughness:
Success in basketball often requires not just physical prowess but also mental toughness. This section delves into how players cultivate resilience and mental strength through the ups and downs. It showcases instances where passion for the game becomes a catalyst for developing a mindset that thrives on challenges, turning setbacks into opportunities for growth.
In "The Love-Hate Relationship," readers witness the raw and unfiltered reality of a basketball player's journey, understanding that the path to greatness is paved with challenges. Through these stories, the enduring passion for the game emerges as a transformative force, enabling players to persevere, learn, and ultimately thrive despite the inevitable obstacles they encounter.

Legacy of Love

In the realm of basketball, certain players transcend the boundaries of their time on the court, leaving behind not only a trail of victories but an enduring legacy of love for the game. These individuals, driven by an unwavering passion, etch their names into the collective memory of basketball enthusiasts. The legacy they leave behind is not just about statistics or accolades but a profound influence that resonates with future generations.

Players who truly love the game become torchbearers for the essence of basketball, embodying values that extend beyond the court. Their commitment, work ethic, and sportsmanship serve as a template for aspiring players, illustrating that success is not solely measured in points scored or championships won but in the genuine love and respect one holds for the sport.

The impact of these players extends far beyond their playing days. Through their actions, both on and off the court, they plant the seeds of inspiration. The next generation of players witnesses not just the dunks, three-pointers, and highlight-reel plays but the sheer joy and dedication with which these basketball icons approached each game.

The legacy of love is evident in the way these players mentor, coach, and engage with the basketball community. Many establish foundations, basketball camps, or charitable initiatives that aim to give back to the sport that has given them so much. By investing time and resources into the development of young talent, they ensure that the flame of passion continues to burn brightly.

Beyond the physical skills, these players impart invaluable lessons about resilience, perseverance, and the importance of embracing challenges. They teach that setbacks are not defeats but opportunities for growth, and that true success lies not just in personal achievements but in the collective triumph of the team.

As the years pass, the legacy of love becomes a guiding light for emerging players. It fosters a culture where the heart and dedication to the game are revered as much as, if not more than, individual prowess. The impact ripples through basketball programs, inspiring coaches to prioritize character development alongside skill enhancement.

In essence, the legacy of love in basketball is a gift that keeps on giving. It is a continuous source of motivation for future athletes, a reminder that the heart and soul poured into the game are what truly elevate it to an art form. These players become immortal not just for their feats on the court but for the indelible mark they leave on the very spirit of basketball itself—a legacy that transcends time and continues to shape the game for generations to come.

In this chapter, we delve into the captivating journeys of basketball legends, whose stories continue to resonate and inspire generations. These icons not only conquered the courts but left an indelible mark on the sport, shaping it into the dynamic and inspiring spectacle we witness today.

Michael Jordan: A Legacy of Greatness

Michael Jordan, widely regarded as the greatest basketball player of all time, etched his name into the annals of sports history through a remarkable journey from a determined young player to a global basketball phenomenon. His story is a testament to resilience, talent, and an unparalleled work ethic that set new standards for excellence in the world of sports.

Early Challenges: The Drive to Succeed:
Michael's journey began in Wilmington, North Carolina, where he faced initial challenges and skepticism about his future in basketball. Cut from his high school team as a sophomore, Jordan's determination and hunger for success fueled an

intense work ethic. He used rejection as motivation, honing his skills and transforming setbacks into stepping stones towards greatness.

The University of North Carolina: Rising Stardom:
Jordan's talent shone brightly during his college years at the University of North Carolina. His game-winning shot in the 1982 NCAA Championship game against Georgetown catapulted him to national prominence. The foundation for his legacy was laid, as his work ethic and competitiveness became evident on the collegiate stage.

Chicago Bulls Era: A Dynasty in the Making:
Selected by the Chicago Bulls as the third overall pick in the 1984 NBA Draft, Jordan quickly became the face of the franchise. Despite early playoff disappointments, his work ethic remained unyielding. Hours of practice, relentless conditioning, and an unmatched desire to win defined his approach. The result was a six-time NBA champion and a player who redefined the parameters of success in professional basketball.

The Flu Game and Beyond: Unyielding Determination:
One of the most iconic moments in Jordan's career came during the 1997 NBA Finals, known as "The Flu Game." Battling illness, he delivered an awe-inspiring performance, showcasing not only his skill but an unyielding determination that has become emblematic of his legacy. This moment encapsulates the indomitable spirit that fueled his success.

Legacy Beyond the Court: Impact on the Sport:
Michael Jordan's influence transcended the basketball court. His impact on the sport's global popularity is immeasurable. From the iconic Air Jordan sneaker line to his ownership of the Charlotte Hornets, Jordan's imprint on the basketball industry endures. His success in blending athletic prowess with charisma transformed the NBA into a global entertainment phenomenon.

Enduring Impact: A Role Model for Aspiring Athletes:

Beyond his numerous accolades, Jordan's legacy is cemented as a role model for aspiring athletes. His relentless pursuit of excellence, dedication to the craft, and ability to perform under pressure continue to inspire generations of basketball players. The phrase "Be Like Mike" extends far beyond a marketing slogan; it embodies the aspirational drive to emulate the greatness of a true sporting icon.

In exploring Michael Jordan's journey, one discovers not just a basketball legend but a symbol of determination, perseverance, and the unwavering pursuit of excellence. His legacy continues to shape the landscape of basketball, leaving an indelible mark on the sport and serving as a timeless source of inspiration for young players around the world.

Kobe Bryant: Mamba Mentality

Kobe Bryant's journey from a precocious young talent to an NBA legend was defined not only by his remarkable skill on the court but by a mindset that transcended the boundaries of the game. This section delves into the intricacies of Kobe's life, exploring the evolution of the "Mamba Mentality" that fueled his pursuit of excellence.

Early Struggles and Determination:
Kobe Bryant's story began with a passion for the game that was evident from a young age. Growing up as the son of former NBA player Joe "Jellybean" Bryant, Kobe faced the challenge of living up to high expectations. Delve into his early struggles, including being the youngest player in the league when he entered the NBA straight out of high school. Explore the criticism and skepticism he faced and how these early challenges forged the foundation of his unyielding determination.

The Evolution of Mamba Mentality:
As Kobe matured in the league, he developed a reputation for unmatched work ethic and an unwavering desire to improve. Examine the turning points in his career, such as his partnership with Shaquille O'Neal and the subsequent

"three-peat" championships with the Los Angeles Lakers. Investigate how these experiences contributed to the development of the "Mamba Mentality" — a philosophy centered around relentless pursuit of greatness, continuous self-improvement, and the ability to perform under pressure.

Championship Triumphs and Leadership:
The chapter further explores Kobe's leadership style and the pivotal role he played in guiding his teams to multiple championships. Analyze key moments, such as his iconic performances in the NBA Finals, and dissect how his mindset influenced those around him. Uncover the meticulous preparation and mental fortitude that became synonymous with the "Mamba Mentality" and set Kobe apart as a leader on and off the court.

Global Impact and Legacy:
The "Mamba Mentality" transcended borders, becoming a global phenomenon and a source of inspiration for athletes across various disciplines. Investigate Kobe's post-basketball career, including his Oscar-winning animated short film "Dear Basketball" and his dedication to coaching and mentoring the next generation. Explore the enduring legacy of the "Mamba Mentality" and how it continues to shape the mindset of aspiring athletes worldwide.

Through an in-depth examination of Kobe Bryant's life and career, this section aims to not only showcase his on-court achievements but also to dissect the mindset that propelled him to greatness. The "Mamba Mentality" serves as a timeless blueprint for aspiring athletes, emphasizing the importance of dedication, resilience, and an unwavering commitment to one's craft.

Bill Russell: Beyond the Court

Bill Russell's impact on the game of basketball is unquestionable, but his legacy extends far beyond the hardwood. Russell emerged as a pivotal figure during a crucial period in American history, using his platform to champion civil rights and effect transformative change.

Born in 1934, Russell faced racial prejudice from an early age, and this experience fueled his determination to not only succeed in basketball but also to make a difference in society. As he rose to prominence with the Boston Celtics in the late 1950s and 1960s, Russell became the first Black coach in NBA history, breaking down racial barriers in a predominantly white league.

Russell's commitment to civil rights became increasingly visible during a time of societal unrest. He wasn't content with being a silent athlete; instead, he embraced his role as a prominent African American figure. Russell spoke out against racial injustice, often at great personal risk, and used his celebrity status to advocate for change.

One of the notable instances of Russell's activism was during the 1963 March on Washington for Jobs and Freedom, where he stood alongside Dr. Martin Luther King Jr. His presence at such a historic event underscored the intersectionality of sports and civil rights, emphasizing that athletes could be agents of change beyond the confines of the arena.

In addition to his activism, Russell's leadership on the court mirrored his commitment to equality off the court. He led the Celtics to numerous championships, showcasing that success could be achieved through teamwork and inclusivity. His ability to foster a sense of unity among his teammates transcended racial boundaries, setting an example for the entire league.

Off the court, Russell continued to influence social change through his writings and public engagements. His autobiography, "Go Up for Glory," offered insights into his experiences and perspectives on race and basketball, contributing to the broader discourse on civil rights in America.

Bill Russell's story, therefore, serves as a testament to the broader impact that sports figures can have on society. By using his platform to challenge racial norms, fight for justice, and break down barriers, Russell not only transformed the landscape of professional basketball but also left an indelible mark on the ongoing struggle for civil rights in the United States. His legacy encourages athletes to recognize the power they possess to effect positive change both on and off the playing field.

Magic Johnson: The Showtime Era

Magic Johnson's career transcended the boundaries of ordinary basketball achievement. In the hallowed halls of the NBA, he carved his niche not just as a player but as the orchestrator of the "Showtime" era with the Los Angeles Lakers. This period, spanning the 1980s, was characterized by a dazzling display of fast breaks, precision passes, and unparalleled excitement on the court—a spectacle that would forever be associated with Magic Johnson.

The Rise of Magic: A Rookie Maestro:
Magic burst onto the NBA scene in 1979 as the first overall pick in the draft, anointed to lead the Lakers to glory. What unfolded was nothing short of spectacular. In his rookie season, he showcased an otherworldly blend of size, skill, and court vision that belied his youth. His infectious smile and charismatic demeanor endeared him to fans, teammates, and opponents alike.
Showtime Unleashed: Magic's Playmaking Prowess:
Under Magic's guidance, the Lakers embraced a style of play that was revolutionary at the time. Showtime was characterized by lightning-fast transitions, no-look passes, and an up-tempo pace that left defenses scrambling. Magic, often playing at the point guard position, became the master conductor of this symphony, orchestrating fast breaks with a flair that transformed every game into a spectacle.

The Rivalry with Larry Bird: A Basketball Drama:
The rivalry between Magic Johnson and Larry Bird became the stuff of basketball legend. The clash between the Lakers and the Boston Celtics in the NBA Finals during the 1980s was a captivating narrative that elevated the league's popularity. Magic's battles with Bird transcended competition; they symbolized the epitome of sportsmanship and mutual respect, showcasing Magic's leadership qualities both on and off the court.

Leadership and Charisma: Magic's Unique Presence
Beyond statistics and highlight-reel plays, Magic's impact was deeply rooted in his leadership and charisma. As the team's floor general, he commanded respect with an inclusive leadership style, involving every player in the action. His ability to elevate his teammates' performances and create a cohesive unit was instrumental in the Lakers' success.

Championship Glory: A Hallmark of Showtime:
Magic Johnson led the Lakers to five NBA championships during the 1980s, cementing their status as one of the greatest dynasties in NBA history. The team's success was a testament to Magic's ability to perform in clutch moments and elevate his game when it mattered most.

Legacy Beyond the Court: Entrepreneurship and Impact:
Magic's influence extended beyond his playing days. His transition into entrepreneurship showcased a different facet of his multifaceted personality. Post-retirement, Magic became a successful businessman, owning a stake in the Los Angeles Lakers and contributing to various philanthropic endeavors. His impact on the community and the game itself solidified his status as a living legend.

In exploring Magic Johnson's journey during the Showtime era, we witness not only a basketball maestro but a cultural icon whose impact reverberates through the annals of the sport. His charisma, leadership, and unmatched skills continue to inspire generations, making Magic Johnson an enduring symbol of basketball excellence.

Larry Bird: Precision and Passion

Larry Bird, a name synonymous with basketball greatness, emerged as one of the most iconic figures in the sport's history. Born on December 7, 1956, in West Baden Springs, Indiana, Bird's journey from the small-town courts to the grand stage of the NBA is a testament to his unparalleled precision and unwavering passion for the game.

Early Days and College Brilliance:
Growing up in the heartland of basketball, Bird developed a love for the game at an early age. His talents became evident during his college years at Indiana State University, where he led the Sycamores to the NCAA Championship game against Magic Johnson's Michigan State Spartans in 1979, creating the foundation for a historic NBA rivalry.

Rivalry with Magic Johnson:
The Larry Bird-Magic Johnson rivalry is the stuff of basketball legend. It began in college and reached its zenith in the NBA, where Bird's Boston Celtics and Magic's Los Angeles Lakers clashed in a series of epic Finals throughout the 1980s. This rivalry not only defined an era but elevated the NBA to new heights of popularity.

Delving into the intricacies of this rivalry, we uncover the competitive fire that fueled both players. Bird's precision on the court, marked by his deadly shooting accuracy and basketball IQ, made him a force to be reckoned with. The battles between the Celtics and the Lakers were not just contests of athleticism but also strategic showdowns between two basketball maestros.

Precision Personified:
Larry Bird's game was a masterclass in precision. His shooting stroke was impeccable, and his ability to read the game and anticipate plays set him apart. Bird's precision extended beyond scoring; it manifested in his passing, rebounding, and defensive maneuvers. His court vision allowed him to orchestrate plays with a surgeon's precision, earning him the nickname "Larry Legend."

Passion for Victory:
What defined Bird's legacy was not just his precision but the unyielding passion he brought to every game. He was known for his relentless work ethic, often arriving at the gym before sunrise to hone his skills. Bird's passion for victory was contagious, elevating the performance of his teammates and inspiring a generation of basketball enthusiasts.

Enduring Legacy:
Larry Bird's impact on the NBA transcends statistics and championships. His legacy lies in the indomitable spirit with which he played the game. The three-time NBA champion, three-time MVP, and 12-time All-Star left an enduring mark on the sport, influencing subsequent generations of players who sought to emulate his precision, passion, and dedication.

Even in retirement, Bird continued to contribute to the game, serving as an executive and playing a pivotal role in the success of the Indiana Pacers. Larry Bird's story is a narrative of excellence, resilience, and an enduring love for the game that continues to inspire basketball enthusiasts worldwide. The precision and passion that defined Larry Bird's career have etched his name in the annals of basketball history, ensuring that the legend of Larry Bird will endure for generations to come.

Tim Duncan: The Quiet Dominance

Tim Duncan's career stands as a testament to the power of quiet excellence, a narrative that transcends the flashy and resonates with the enduring qualities that define greatness. From the Virgin Islands to the hallowed courts of the NBA, Duncan's journey is a tale of humility, consistency, and fundamental mastery that etched his name among the greatest power forwards in the history of the league.

Early Years and Collegiate Stardom:
Born and raised in the Virgin Islands, Tim Duncan's introduction to basketball was marked by a raw talent that caught the attention of scouts. His journey continued at Wake Forest University, where his skills flourished, earning him accolades and recognition as a dominant force in collegiate basketball. Even then, Duncan's approach to the game was characterized by a quiet determination and a commitment to the fundamentals.

San Antonio Spurs Dynasty:
Drafted by the San Antonio Spurs in 1997, Tim Duncan's arrival heralded the beginning of an era of sustained success for the franchise. His partnership with

coach Gregg Popovich became the bedrock of the Spurs' dynasty, a model of consistency in an ever-evolving league. Duncan's quiet leadership style, marked by leading by example, set the tone for the team's culture.

Fundamentals Over Flash:
Duncan's game was defined by its simplicity and efficiency. The bank shot became his trademark, a move executed with such precision that it became nearly impossible to defend. While other stars embraced highlight-reel plays, Duncan's brilliance lay in his mastery of the basics – impeccable footwork, a reliable mid-range jumper, and a defensive prowess that anchored the Spurs.

Quiet Leadership:
In an era of outspoken superstars, Duncan's leadership style was a refreshing departure. He wasn't one to seek the limelight or engage in flashy antics. Instead, he led through his work ethic, resilience, and a commitment to team success. His humility resonated in the locker room, fostering an atmosphere of collective purpose.

Championships and Legacy:
Tim Duncan's impact on the court was most vividly illustrated by the Spurs' championship successes. His stoic demeanor and unyielding focus guided the team to five NBA championships. Each title reinforced the idea that success could be achieved through a steady, unassuming approach, a stark contrast to the more flamboyant narratives prevalent in the league.

Beyond Basketball:
Off the court, Duncan's philanthropy and community involvement further solidified his legacy. His quiet demeanor extended to his personal life, where he shied away from the spotlight, choosing instead to let his actions speak louder than words.

Tim Duncan's career wasn't defined by the roar of the crowd or the dazzling highlights. Instead, it was a symphony of consistency, humility, and fundamental brilliance. His quiet dominance left an indelible mark on the San Antonio Spurs, the NBA, and the hearts of basketball enthusiasts who came to appreciate the beauty of a game played with grace and skill.

Hakeem Olajuwon: The Dream Shake

Hakeem Olajuwon's journey from Nigeria to the pinnacle of NBA greatness is a story of dedication, resilience, and the relentless pursuit of excellence. Born in Lagos, Nigeria, Olajuwon's early exposure to basketball was limited, but his raw talent quickly became apparent. His incredible height, agility, and determination set the stage for a remarkable career that would revolutionize the role of a center in the NBA.

As a college player at the University of Houston, Olajuwon's skills rapidly developed under the guidance of legendary coach Guy Lewis. His shot-blocking prowess, rebounding ability, and offensive skills earned him acclaim, leading the Houston Cougars to consecutive NCAA Championship appearances in 1983 and 1984. The "Phi Slama Jama" era showcased Olajuwon's dominance and marked the beginning of his ascent to basketball stardom.

The pivotal moment in Olajuwon's career came when he was selected as the first overall pick in the 1984 NBA Draft by the Houston Rockets. The transition from collegiate success to the professional stage was seamless for Olajuwon, who quickly established himself as one of the premier centers in the league.

At the heart of Olajuwon's offensive repertoire was the legendary "Dream Shake" move. The Dream Shake was a mesmerizing combination of footwork, fakes, and fluidity that left defenders bewildered. Olajuwon's ability to pivot, spin, and create space with finesse redefined the expectations for a center's offensive game. The Dream Shake became a signature move, a symbol of Olajuwon's artistry on the court and a nightmare for opposing defenses.

The Dream Shake wasn't just a move; it was a testament to Olajuwon's unparalleled work ethic. Hours of practice refining his footwork and mastering the subtleties of the move reflected his commitment to constant improvement. Whether facing double teams or defensive giants, Olajuwon's skillful execution of the Dream Shake showcased his ability to rise above adversity.

Beyond his on-court excellence, Olajuwon's journey from Nigeria to the NBA exemplified the global nature of basketball. His success inspired a generation of international players to pursue their dreams in the NBA. Olajuwon's story illustrated that talent knows no borders, and hard work can overcome any obstacle.

As the centerpiece of the Houston Rockets, Olajuwon led his team to back-to-back NBA championships in 1994 and 1995. His impact extended beyond individual accolades, as he earned numerous All-Star selections, MVP honors, and Defensive Player of the Year awards. Hakeem Olajuwon's legacy endures not only for his contributions to the game but also for the enduring inspiration he provides to aspiring players worldwide. His journey is a testament to the transformative power of dedication, hard work, and the pursuit of one's dreams in the world of basketball.

Wilt Chamberlain: Record-Breaking Giant

Wilt Chamberlain's name is synonymous with basketball greatness, and his astonishing career remains etched in the annals of the sport. Born in 1936, Chamberlain soared to unprecedented heights, leaving an indelible mark on the game with his remarkable statistical achievements and on-court dominance.

Dominance in Numbers:
Wilt Chamberlain's statistical achievements are nothing short of legendary. During the 1961-62 NBA season, he achieved one of the most iconic feats in basketball history by scoring an average of 50.4 points per game—a record that still stands to this day. His ability to score at will and his dominance on the boards revolutionized the center position, setting standards that many have aspired to but few have achieved.

Chamberlain's dominance was not confined to scoring alone. He holds the record for the most points scored in a single game, an astounding 100-point performance on March 2, 1962, while playing for the Philadelphia Warriors against the New York Knicks. This historic achievement showcased not only his scoring prowess but also his unparalleled physicality and skill on the court.

Rebounding and Defensive Prowess:
Beyond scoring, Chamberlain's rebounding prowess was equally awe-inspiring. He led the league in rebounds for 11 seasons and holds the record for the highest single-season rebounding average at 27.2 rebounds per game during the 1960-61 season. His combination of size, athleticism, and timing made him a force to be reckoned with on both ends of the court.

Defensively, Chamberlain was a formidable presence. His shot-blocking ability and rim protection were ahead of his time, influencing the way future generations of centers approached defense. His impact was not just about the numbers; it was about the fear he instilled in opponents and the way he fundamentally altered the strategies of opposing teams.

Enduring Legacy:
Wilt Chamberlain's legacy extends far beyond the record books. His impact on modern basketball can be seen in the evolution of the game itself. The emphasis on athleticism, the importance of dominant centers, and the pursuit of individual greatness can all be traced back to Chamberlain's influence.
His statistical achievements are not just records; they are a testament to the heights that a player can reach with unparalleled skill and determination. Chamberlain's legacy lives on through the players who have followed in his footsteps, each one striving to achieve greatness and etch their name in the storied history of the sport.

Influence on Modern Basketball:
Chamberlain's impact is felt in the playing style of modern centers who seek to emulate his versatility and dominance. The archetype of the dominant big man owes much to Chamberlain's contributions, and his legacy continues to inspire players to push the boundaries of what is possible on the basketball court.

In conclusion, Wilt Chamberlain's record-breaking career goes beyond the numbers; it symbolizes the epitome of basketball excellence. His influence reverberates through the decades, reminding us that true greatness leaves an enduring legacy that shapes the very essence of the game. Wilt Chamberlain, the record-breaking giant, will forever stand as a towering figure in the history of basketball.

Kareem Abdul-Jabbar: Skyhook and Social Activism

Kareem Abdul-Jabbar, standing at an impressive 7 feet 2 inches, wasn't just a towering figure on the basketball court; he was a force to be reckoned with both in the game and in the realm of social activism.

On-Court Dominance: The Unstoppable Skyhook:
Kareem's on-court prowess was epitomized by his signature move—the skyhook. This seemingly indefensible shot, executed with grace and precision, contributed significantly to his status as the NBA's all-time leading scorer. Abdul-Jabbar's skyhook was not just a move; it was a symbol of his unparalleled skill, versatility, and dominance on the court. Opponents struggled to counter this seemingly unstoppable shot, solidifying his legacy as one of the greatest centers in the history of the game.

Beyond Basketball: A Champion for Change:
While Kareem Abdul-Jabbar's contributions to basketball are unquestionable, his impact off the court is equally profound. Recognizing the platform and influence bestowed upon him, Abdul-Jabbar became a vocal advocate for social justice and civil rights during a turbulent era in American history.

In the 1960s and 1970s, when the nation grappled with issues of racial inequality and injustice, Kareem Abdul-Jabbar was at the forefront of the conversation. He used his position as a prominent athlete to address societal issues, speaking out against racism and advocating for equality. His eloquent and thoughtful commentary on matters beyond basketball demonstrated that athletes could be more than just entertainers—they could be agents of change.

Social Activism: An Unyielding Voice:
Abdul-Jabbar's activism was not limited to words; he took tangible actions to effect change. He was actively involved in various community initiatives, working to improve educational opportunities and promote social equality. His commitment to social justice extended beyond his playing days, solidifying his reputation as a lifelong advocate for positive societal change.

During an era when athletes were sometimes hesitant to engage in political discourse, Kareem Abdul-Jabbar fearlessly used his platform to address systemic issues. His influence transcended basketball arenas, reaching into living rooms across the nation. Through his actions, Abdul-Jabbar inspired a generation of athletes to recognize the power they held to shape not only the sports landscape but also the broader social and political landscape.

Legacy: The Skyhook and Social Change:
Kareem Abdul-Jabbar's enduring legacy is a dual one—marked by his unparalleled achievements on the basketball court and his unwavering commitment to social justice. The skyhook remains an iconic symbol of basketball excellence, while Abdul-Jabbar's activism serves as a reminder that athletes can be catalysts for positive change. His story illustrates that true greatness extends beyond athletic achievements, emphasizing the importance of using one's influence to make a lasting impact on the world. In celebrating Abdul-Jabbar's legacy, we celebrate not only a basketball legend but a champion for justice and equality.

Shaquille O'Neal: Larger Than Life

Shaquille O'Neal, often referred to simply as "Shaq," emerged as a colossal force both on and off the basketball court. In this segment, we unravel the layers of his larger-than-life persona, shedding light on his dominating presence in the paint, his infectious charisma, and the profound impact he made on popular culture.

Dominance in the Paint:

Shaq's physical prowess was nothing short of extraordinary. Standing at a towering 7 feet 1 inch and weighing in at over 300 pounds, he was an imposing figure in the paint. His combination of size, strength, and agility made him nearly unstoppable close to the basket. Explore the moments of sheer dominance, the thunderous dunks, and the iconic plays that solidified Shaq's reputation as one of the most dominant centers in NBA history.

Charismatic Personality:
Beyond his athletic abilities, Shaq's charisma set him apart. Known for his engaging smile, playful demeanor, and a sense of humor as vast as his physical stature, Shaq endeared himself to fans worldwide. Delve into the off-court moments that showcased his personality, from entertaining interviews to memorable interactions with teammates and opponents. Discover how this larger-than-life personality made Shaq not just a basketball icon but a beloved figure in the world of sports and entertainment.

Impact on Popular Culture:
Shaq's influence transcended the basketball court, reaching deep into popular culture. Explore his foray into music with rap albums, collaborations with renowned artists, and even a brief stint as a DJ. Investigate his ventures in acting and television, including memorable roles in movies and appearances in commercials. Shaq became a household name, and his impact resonated far beyond the realm of sports, making him a cultural phenomenon.

Business Ventures and Philanthropy:
Shaquille O'Neal's success extended into the business world. Examine his diverse business ventures, from investments in technology companies to ownership stakes in major brands. Additionally, explore Shaq's commitment to philanthropy, highlighting his efforts to give back to communities through initiatives that focus on education, healthcare, and social justice.

Legacy and Enduring Impact:
As we reflect on Shaq's illustrious career, explore the lasting impact he has had on the NBA and the sports world as a whole. Discuss his influence on

subsequent generations of players, the continuation of his legacy in various facets of popular culture, and the enduring admiration from fans around the globe.

Through the lens of Shaquille O'Neal's journey, readers are invited to witness the convergence of athleticism, charisma, and cultural influence that defines the essence of a basketball legend. Shaq's story is not just about his accomplishments on the court but the profound and lasting mark he left on the world beyond the hardwood.

Each legend's story serves as a beacon of inspiration for young readers, offering profound insights into the qualities that define true greatness in the world of basketball. The tales of these iconic players go beyond the confines of the court, revealing valuable life lessons that extend far beyond the game itself.

Through the trials and triumphs of Michael Jordan, Kobe Bryant, Bill Russell, Magic Johnson, Larry Bird, Tim Duncan, Hakeem Olajuwon, Wilt Chamberlain, Kareem Abdul-Jabbar, and Shaquille O'Neal, a common thread emerges: the fusion of raw talent, unwavering dedication, and a deep, abiding love for the sport. It's a powerful reminder that achieving greatness is not an overnight feat but a journey fraught with challenges, setbacks, and relentless perseverance.

These legends didn't just rely on their innate abilities; they honed their skills through countless hours of practice and a commitment to continuous improvement. Michael Jordan's infamous work ethic, Kobe Bryant's relentless pursuit of perfection, and Tim Duncan's quiet but unwavering consistency showcase the importance of disciplined training and a never-ending quest for excellence.

Moreover, the stories of Bill Russell, Magic Johnson, and Kareem Abdul-Jabbar emphasize the broader impact athletes can have beyond the court. Their commitment to social justice and community involvement illustrates that true greatness involves not just personal achievement but also a responsibility to contribute positively to society.

As young readers immerse themselves in these narratives, they are invited to reflect on the principles that define success in any endeavor—qualities like resilience, teamwork, leadership, and the courage to overcome adversity. The aim is not merely to idolize these legends but to draw inspiration from their journeys, internalize the values they embodied, and apply these lessons in their own pursuit of excellence.

These profiles are crafted not just for basketball enthusiasts but for anyone seeking inspiration to overcome challenges and strive for greatness in their chosen field. By sharing the stories of these basketball legends, this chapter endeavors to instill a sense of determination, passion, and purpose in the hearts of the next generation of aspiring athletes. Through the lens of these remarkable individuals, young readers are encouraged to dream big, work hard, and, above all, find joy in the journey toward realizing their fullest potential—both on and off the court.

In this chapter, we delve into the captivating stories of young basketball players whose unwavering determination and passion propelled them to pursue their dreams, aiming to make a significant mark in the world of basketball.

Rising from the Streets: The Tale of Jamal Thompson

Jamal Thompson's story is one of resilience and triumph against the odds, a testament to the transformative power of basketball in the face of adversity.
Born and raised in the heart of a tough neighborhood, Jamal's childhood was marked by challenges that would have deterred many. The streets echoed with the struggles of daily life, but amidst the chaos, Jamal discovered the basketball court as a sanctuary—a place where he could channel his energy, dreams, and aspirations.

From an early age, Jamal exhibited an innate talent for the game. The cracked pavement of the neighborhood court became his training ground, and the rhythmic bounce of the ball echoed his determination to rise above his circumstances. Basketball was not merely a sport for Jamal; it was a lifeline, a beacon guiding him through the challenges that surrounded him.

Despite facing economic hardships and a lack of resources, Jamal's passion for the game burned brightly. His neighborhood became a crucible where his skills were honed, and the local courts witnessed the emergence of a young player with exceptional potential. Jamal's commitment to basketball was unwavering; after school and on weekends, he could be found on the court, perfecting his shots and refining his moves.

Word of Jamal's talent spread beyond the boundaries of his neighborhood, catching the attention of coaches and scouts who frequented local tournaments. Recognizing his potential, they saw in Jamal a player with not only skill but also the tenacity to overcome adversity. It was through these connections that Jamal's journey took an unexpected turn.

A scholarship to a prestigious basketball academy became Jamal's ticket out of his challenging environment. This opportunity was not just a pathway to hone his skills at a higher level but a chance for a better life. The academy provided a supportive environment, quality coaching, and exposure to a broader basketball community.

As Jamal stepped onto the courts of the academy, he carried with him the hopes and dreams of his neighborhood. His journey from the cracked pavements of the streets to the polished floors of the academy was a beacon of inspiration for young players facing similar challenges. Jamal's success proved that talent knows no boundaries, and with dedication and perseverance, one can rise above even the toughest circumstances.

Jamal Thompson's story became a source of pride for his community, an illustration of the transformative power of basketball, and a reminder that dreams can be realized, no matter where you come from. His tale continues to inspire young players, showing them that the journey from the streets to success is paved with resilience, hard work, and an unwavering belief in oneself.

Small Town, Big Dreams: Maria Rodriguez's Journey

In the heart of a forgotten small town, where basketball courts were weathered and forgotten, Maria Rodriguez emerged as an unexpected beacon of hope. Basketball was a mere echo in the narrow streets, where dreams seemed to dissipate like mist. Maria, however, refused to succumb to the limitations of her surroundings. Her story would redefine what was possible for the young girls of her community.

Raised in a family that struggled to make ends meet, Maria discovered her love for basketball early on. With a makeshift hoop attached to the side of her family's modest home, she spent endless hours practicing, perfecting her dribbles, and honing her shooting skills. The passion for the game burned fiercely within her, a flame that refused to be extinguished by the challenges of her humble beginnings.

As Maria entered her teenage years, the local basketball scene remained dominated by boys. The town, steeped in tradition, held tightly to the belief that sports were a male domain. Undeterred by societal expectations, Maria approached the coach of the boys' basketball team, expressing her desire to play. Skepticism filled the air as eyebrows were raised, but Maria's determination spoke louder than any preconceived notions.

Her journey on the boys' team was marked by grit and resilience. At first met with resistance and skepticism from teammates, Maria's skills quickly silenced doubters. She dribbled past defenders with finesse, sank three-pointers with precision, and displayed an innate understanding of the game that transcended gender norms. The town began to take notice.

Maria's presence on the court became a catalyst for change. Young girls who had never considered basketball as an option found inspiration in her fearlessness. Maria's story started to reshape the narrative, challenging the deeply ingrained gender stereotypes that had constrained the dreams of aspiring female athletes in the town.

Community support began to swell around Maria. Local businesses sponsored the team, and the once-neglected basketball courts were revitalized. The town embraced the idea that talent knew no gender, and Maria became a symbol of possibility for every young girl who dared to dream beyond the confines of societal expectations.

Word of Maria's achievements spread beyond the town's borders. She received invitations to regional tournaments, catching the attention of scouts and college recruiters. Maria's journey from a small town where basketball was an afterthought to a prospect on the national stage became a testament to the transformative power of pursuing one's dreams, regardless of where you start.

Maria Rodriguez not only broke through gender barriers on the court but also became an advocate for equal opportunities in sports. Her journey opened doors for young girls, proving that passion, skill, and determination could pave the way for a brighter, more inclusive future in the world of basketball. The small town, once resigned to anonymity, became a symbol of resilience and possibility, all thanks to one girl who dared to dream big.

The Refugee's Triumph: Ahmed's Story

Ahmed's story is one of resilience, hope, and the transformative power of basketball in the face of unimaginable adversity. As a young refugee displaced by conflict, Ahmed's early years were marked by the harsh realities of war, loss, and displacement. Forced to leave behind his home and everything familiar, he found himself in a new and unfamiliar land, struggling to adapt to a life vastly different from what he had known.

Amidst the challenges of adjusting to a foreign culture and grappling with a language barrier, Ahmed discovered a refuge on the basketball court. The rhythmic bounce of the ball, the squeak of sneakers on the hardwood, and the camaraderie with fellow players became a source of solace and hope in the midst of uncertainty. Basketball became more than just a game for Ahmed; it became a lifeline, a means of expression, and a pathway to a brighter future.

Despite the initial struggles, Ahmed's innate talent on the court did not go unnoticed. His agility, determination, and ability to seamlessly communicate through the language of basketball captured the attention of coaches and fellow players alike. Through countless hours of practice, he honed his skills and demonstrated that the love for the game could transcend cultural and linguistic barriers.

Ahmed's journey is a testament to the universal language of basketball—a language that speaks of teamwork, passion, and the pursuit of excellence. As he navigated the challenges of adapting to a new life, the basketball court became a microcosm of unity, where differences faded away, and shared goals took precedence.

The pivotal moment in Ahmed's story came when he was offered a spot on a local team, breaking down the barriers that often accompany displacement and offering him a chance to rebuild his life. His journey from a war-torn home to the basketball courts of a foreign land is a poignant example of the power of dreams. Ahmed not only found a new home within the confines of the court but also showcased the transformative potential of sports in the lives of those who have faced unimaginable hardships.

Ultimately, Ahmed's triumph serves as an inspiration to young readers, illustrating that, regardless of circumstances, the pursuit of one's dreams and the love for a sport can act as a beacon of hope, resilience, and a testament to the indomitable human spirit.

Overcoming Physical Challenges: Emily's Victory

Emily's journey is a testament to the extraordinary resilience of the human spirit in the face of seemingly insurmountable physical challenges. Born with a congenital condition that affected her mobility, Emily could have easily succumbed to societal expectations and abandoned her dreams of engaging in competitive sports. However, her deep-seated love for basketball and an indomitable spirit propelled her towards a path of triumph and inspiration.

From an early age, Emily found solace on the basketball court. The rhythmic dribbling of the ball, the squeak of sneakers against the hardwood, and the camaraderie of teammates became her sanctuary. Despite the physical hurdles she faced, Emily's determination to be a part of the game she loved remained unwavering.

Emily's family played a pivotal role in nurturing her passion. Encouraged by her parents, who recognized the spark in their daughter's eyes whenever she held a basketball, Emily began her journey. Early on, she faced skepticism and doubt from those who questioned her ability to compete at the same level as her peers. However, Emily's persistent spirit and unyielding resolve gradually turned skeptics into supporters.

Her journey through local leagues and school competitions was marked by countless hours of extra practice and a fierce commitment to honing her skills. Emily's coaches, impressed not only by her dedication but also by her ability to adapt and overcome physical challenges, became instrumental in her development. They tailored training routines to suit her unique needs, fostering an inclusive and supportive environment.

As Emily's prowess on the court grew, so did her impact beyond the game. She became a source of inspiration for her teammates, demonstrating that true strength emanates from the mind and heart, transcending physical limitations. Emily's story began to resonate with a broader audience, reaching beyond the basketball community. Schools, local media, and even national outlets began to share her narrative, turning her into a symbol of resilience and determination.

Ultimately, Emily's journey culminated in a significant moment — she earned a spot on the national adaptive basketball team, representing her country on an international stage. Her inclusion not only broke barriers for athletes with physical challenges but also showcased the inclusive nature of the basketball community.

Emily's victory extends far beyond the court; it speaks to the power of self-belief, the unwavering support of loved ones, and the transformative potential of sports.

Through her triumph over physical challenges, Emily became more than an athlete; she became a beacon of hope, proving that the human spirit can soar to incredible heights, even in the face of adversity. Her story continues to inspire aspiring athletes and reminds us all of the boundless possibilities within the inclusive embrace of the basketball community.

From Playground to Pros: The Phenom, Jake Mitchell

As the sun dipped below the horizon, casting long shadows across the weathered concrete courts of Jake Mitchell's childhood neighborhood, a journey of destiny began. It was on these gritty playgrounds that Jake first gripped a basketball, his small hands barely able to contain the dreams that were about to unfold.

Born into modest surroundings, Jake's love for the game burned brightly from an early age. The rhythmic echoes of dribbles, the thud of sneakers against the asphalt, and the chorus of laughter filled the air as Jake honed his skills. Despite the makeshift hoops and cracked pavement, this was where he discovered the magic of the game that would shape his destiny.

His raw talent did not go unnoticed. Scouts from local high schools began to whisper about the kid with lightning-quick crossovers and an uncanny ability to sink three-pointers. However, what set Jake apart wasn't just his innate skill; it was the relentless work ethic that fueled his every move. Long after the sun had set, he could be found alone on the court, perfecting his shot, refining his handles, and dreaming of a future beyond the neighborhood courts.

As the years unfolded, Jake's journey took a pivotal turn when he earned a scholarship to a prestigious college basketball program. The transition from the familiar playgrounds to the polished courts of a renowned institution was both thrilling and challenging. Yet, Jake's commitment to his craft remained unyielding. Late-night practice sessions and early morning workouts became his routine, a testament to the discipline that would ultimately set him on the path to greatness.

His college career became the stuff of legends. Jake led his team to championships, earning accolades and catching the eye of professional scouts.

Yet, amidst the growing recognition and the allure of the pros, Jake never lost sight of the values instilled on those neighborhood playgrounds. He remained grounded, staying true to the passion that ignited his journey.

Finally, the long-awaited draft night arrived. The culmination of years of dedication and hard work materialized as Jake Mitchell's name echoed through the arena, announcing his entry into the professional league. The kid from the playgrounds had evolved into a phenom, but his story was more than just individual success; it was a roadmap for aspiring young players.

Jake's journey, from the humble beginnings of playground dreams to the grand stage of professional basketball, resonates as a beacon of inspiration. His story serves as a testament to the transformative power of dedication, hard work, and unwavering passion. For every aspiring young player who dribbles a ball on a weathered court, Jake Mitchell's tale provides not just a roadmap but a profound assurance that, with perseverance, dreams can indeed evolve from playground fantasies to professional realities.

Conclusion:

Each of these compelling stories serves as a powerful testament to the enduring spirit of dreams within the world of basketball. They vividly illustrate that the pursuit of greatness on the court is not confined by age, background, or circumstances. Instead, it is fueled by an unwavering passion, resilience, and an unyielding belief in one's abilities.

In Jamal Thompson's journey, we witness the transformative power of basketball as a vehicle for change. His story echoes the sentiment that talent can emerge from the most unexpected places, breaking the shackles of socioeconomic challenges and providing a pathway for those who dare to dream.

Maria Rodriguez's triumph challenges the conventional norms associated with gender and sports. By defying stereotypes in her small town, Maria not only showcases her individual skill but becomes a beacon of inspiration for aspiring young girls who dream of making their mark in the world of basketball. Her story reinforces the idea that the court is a space for all who love the game, regardless of gender or societal expectations.

Ahmed's experience as a refugee emphasizes the universal language of basketball. Despite facing displacement and the trauma of conflict, the sport becomes a means of integration and healing. His journey exemplifies the unifying force of basketball, transcending borders and backgrounds, and demonstrating that the pursuit of dreams can flourish even in the face of adversity.

Emily's victory over physical challenges resonates with the inclusivity of the basketball community. Her story becomes a symbol of empowerment for those who might feel constrained by physical limitations, illustrating that the love for the game and a determined spirit can overcome any obstacle.

Finally, Jake Mitchell's rise from the playgrounds to the professional stage epitomizes the classic American dream. His journey underscores the timeless values of hard work, dedication, and perseverance, showcasing that regardless of one's starting point, the path to greatness is paved with commitment and a genuine love for the sport.
Collectively, these young players' stories serve as beacons of inspiration, illuminating the path for anyone shooting for their dreams in the world of basketball. They invite aspiring athletes to look beyond the limitations society may impose and to embrace the transformative potential of the game. By showcasing the diverse backgrounds and unique challenges these players faced, these narratives instill the belief that dreams are not merely aspirations but powerful catalysts for change and achievement on the basketball court and beyond.

In the realm of basketball, true greatness extends beyond the court's hardwood surface. This chapter unveils the stories of remarkable players who seamlessly blended their on-court prowess with achievements in life, emphasizing the significance of maintaining a well-rounded existence.

Magic Johnson: A Business Maestro

The court was where Earvin "Magic" Johnson wove spells with his unmatched basketball finesse, but his impact extended far beyond the confines of the game. Magic's journey into a second act was marked by a seamless transition that spotlighted not only his on-court legacy but also his formidable business acumen.

In the twilight of his playing career, Magic didn't merely retire; he embarked on a new chapter as a shrewd entrepreneur. The first pages of this chapter saw him acquiring ownership stakes in the very team that had become synonymous with his greatness—the Los Angeles Lakers. This move wasn't merely symbolic; it was a testament to Magic's commitment to the sport and the city that had witnessed his rise to stardom.

However, Magic's vision transcended the basketball court. With an astute eye for opportunities, he diversified his portfolio and ventured into urban development, transforming neglected neighborhoods into thriving centers of commerce. His commitment to revitalizing communities was not just a business strategy; it reflected a deep-rooted belief in using his success to uplift those around him.

Magic's entry into the business world wasn't without challenges. Yet, much like his ability to navigate through a tight defense, he displayed resilience and strategic thinking. The theaters where he once showcased his dazzling no-look passes became boardrooms where he made calculated decisions, proving that the skills acquired on the court were transferable to the business arena.

As Magic's investments flourished, so did his reputation as a savvy businessman. Beyond the financial gains, his success became a beacon of inspiration for aspiring entrepreneurs, particularly from underprivileged backgrounds. Magic's story resonated with the belief that with hard work, determination, and strategic thinking, anyone could achieve success beyond their initial arena of expertise.
In essence, Magic Johnson's off-court triumphs mirrored the grace and precision of his basketball performances. Whether orchestrating a fast break or revitalizing urban landscapes, Magic demonstrated that the magic wasn't confined to the basketball court—it was a force that could shape and transform the world outside, leaving an indelible mark on the realms of both sports and business.

Tim Duncan: The Silent Philanthropist

Tim Duncan, celebrated for his calm demeanor and dominant presence on the basketball court, revealed a depth of character that extended far beyond the confines of the arena. Nicknamed "The Big Fundamental" for his precise and fundamental playing style, Duncan's impact reached beyond his achievements in the game.
In the post-retirement chapter of his life, Tim Duncan became a beacon of hope and support through his philanthropic endeavors. The establishment of the Tim Duncan Foundation marked a pivotal moment in his journey, demonstrating an unwavering commitment to making a positive difference in the lives of others.

The Tim Duncan Foundation: A Catalyst for Change

Quietly, without fanfare or seeking the spotlight, Duncan utilized his foundation as a powerful instrument for change. The foundation's mission echoed Duncan's values and priorities, with a focus on three key pillars: health initiatives, youth education, and disaster relief efforts.

1. Health Initiatives: Transforming Lives

Tim Duncan's passion for health extended beyond the demands of the basketball court. The foundation actively supported initiatives aimed at improving health outcomes, particularly in underserved communities. From partnering with healthcare organizations to fund critical medical research to facilitating access to essential health services, Duncan's commitment to promoting well-being touched countless lives.

2. Youth Education: Empowering the Future

Recognizing the transformative power of education, the Tim Duncan Foundation invested significantly in youth education programs. Scholarships, mentorship initiatives, and the development of educational resources became integral components of Duncan's efforts to empower the next generation. By fostering a love for learning and providing educational opportunities, he aimed to break down barriers and open doors for young minds to flourish.

3. Hurricane Relief Efforts: A Helping Hand in Times of Crisis

Tim Duncan's philanthropic spirit shone brightly in the face of adversity. When hurricanes and natural disasters struck, the foundation mobilized resources to provide immediate relief and long-term support to affected communities. Duncan's hands-on involvement in relief efforts showcased a genuine empathy for those facing hardships, reinforcing the notion that athletes possess the ability to be powerful agents of positive change.

In the world of philanthropy, Tim Duncan's contributions were characterized by humility, authenticity, and a sincere desire to uplift others. His legacy extended beyond the hardwood, leaving an indelible mark on the lives of those he touched through the Tim Duncan Foundation. Through his actions, Duncan exemplified the profound impact that athletes can have off the court, reminding the world that true success is measured not just in points and rebounds but in the positive difference one makes in the lives of others.

Kareem Abdul-Jabbar: Literary Giant

Kareem Abdul-Jabbar's journey from the basketball court to the world of literature is a testament to the depth of his intellectual curiosity and his commitment to making a positive impact beyond the realm of sports. Widely known for his iconic skyhook shot and unmatched dominance on the basketball court, Abdul-Jabbar's transition into a literary giant was both unexpected and inspiring.

Retiring with an illustrious NBA career as the all-time leading scorer, Abdul-Jabbar embarked on a new chapter in his life, demonstrating that his contributions to society were not limited to his athletic achievements. His foray into literature was marked by a series of thought-provoking essays, memoirs, and books that delved into various aspects of American history, culture, and social justice.

Abdul-Jabbar's first major literary work, "Giant Steps," published in 1983, provided readers with insights into his life as a basketball superstar and his experiences as an African American athlete. This marked the beginning of his exploration into writing as a means of self-expression and social commentary. Over the years, he continued to expand his literary repertoire, addressing issues such as race, religion, and politics with eloquence and depth.
As a cultural ambassador, Abdul-Jabbar used his platform to bridge gaps and foster understanding between communities. His writings often tackled complex issues with a blend of historical context and personal anecdotes, encouraging readers to reflect on the interconnectedness of society. Beyond the written word,

he engaged in public speaking engagements and interviews, further cementing his role as a thoughtful advocate for unity and equality.

One of Abdul-Jabbar's notable literary works is "On the Shoulders of Giants," a compelling exploration of the Harlem Renaissance and its impact on African American culture. In this book, he not only celebrated the contributions of unsung heroes but also shed light on the historical challenges faced by marginalized communities. By weaving together history, culture, and his personal reflections, Abdul-Jabbar showcased the power of storytelling to inspire change and foster understanding.

Abdul-Jabbar's multifaceted success as a literary figure, cultural ambassador, and social justice advocate serves as a beacon for athletes and individuals alike. His transition from the basketball court to the world of literature underscores the importance of nurturing diverse interests and using one's platform to contribute meaningfully to societal conversations. In doing so, Kareem Abdul-Jabbar exemplifies the notion that true success extends far beyond the confines of any single arena.

Chris Paul: A Leader On and Off the Court

Chris Paul, recognized for his leadership skills on the court, extended his influence to community service. His commitment to philanthropy, particularly in education and social justice, exemplifies the impact an athlete can have on society. Paul's dedication to uplifting his community serves as a testament to the positive force basketball players can be beyond their playing days.

Grant Hill: Balancing Basketball and Broadcasting

Grant Hill's journey from the hardwood to the broadcast booth is a testament to the versatility and adaptability inherent in some of the basketball world's most iconic figures. As a player, Hill dazzled fans with his on-court finesse, showcasing an extraordinary combination of athleticism, basketball IQ, and leadership skills. However, what sets him apart is not just his playing legacy but also his seamless transition into the realm of sports broadcasting.

After concluding his illustrious NBA career, Hill seamlessly shifted gears, choosing to stay connected to the game he loves by delving into the world of sports commentary. His transition was not just a change in profession but a continuation of his deep passion for basketball. Hill brought a unique perspective to the broadcast booth, drawing from his extensive playing experience to provide insightful analysis and insider commentary.

Hill's ability to articulate the intricacies of the game surpassed expectations. His commentary was not merely a recounting of events but a thoughtful dissection of plays, strategies, and the emotional nuances that make basketball more than just a sport. Whether breaking down a buzzer-beater or analyzing a defensive scheme, Hill's articulate and engaging style made him a standout in the world of sports broadcasting.

What makes Grant Hill's journey particularly inspiring is the way he leveraged his knowledge and passion for the game to excel in a completely different arena. It wasn't just about reminiscing on his playing days; it was about translating the deep understanding he gained as a player into meaningful insights for viewers. This transition showcased the intellectual depth that many athletes possess, often overshadowed by their physical prowess on the court.

In the broadcast booth, Hill became a storyteller, weaving narratives that went beyond the scoreline. His commentary not only appealed to seasoned basketball enthusiasts but also served as an educational tool for those new to the sport. By doing so, Hill expanded the reach of basketball, bringing its beauty and complexity to a broader audience.

Grant Hill's successful foray into sports broadcasting serves as an inspiration for aspiring athletes to recognize the wealth of opportunities that exist beyond their playing careers. It exemplifies the idea that the love for the game can manifest in various forms, and there is immense potential for athletes to contribute meaningfully to the sport even after hanging up their jerseys. Hill's journey underscores the importance of embracing change, adapting to new challenges, and finding fulfillment in diverse arenas while staying connected to the essence of what initially fueled one's passion.

Conclusion: A Slam Dunk in Life

The narratives of Magic Johnson, Tim Duncan, Kareem Abdul-Jabbar, Chris Paul, and Grant Hill illuminate a profound truth that extends far beyond the basketball arena. Their journeys reveal that success is not confined to the number of points scored, championships won, or records broken. Instead, it's a symphony of achievements played on the grand stage of life, harmonizing personal passions, community impact, and professional excellence.
These basketball icons, through their diversified successes, underscore the importance of a holistic approach to life. They are living proof that greatness transcends the confines of the court, seeping into the fabric of society, culture, and philanthropy. In navigating their post-playing careers, they demonstrated that the journey doesn't conclude with the final buzzer; rather, it evolves into a new and dynamic chapter.

The ability to excel in multiple domains—be it entrepreneurship, philanthropy, literature, broadcasting, or social activism—defines the essence of true success. It's a resounding declaration that one's impact can extend far beyond the painted lines of a basketball court. This realization serves as an invaluable lesson for aspiring athletes, encouraging them to view their athletic careers not as finite chapters but as springboards to multifaceted, purpose-driven lives.

The inspiration drawn from these stories is not limited to the realm of sports. It becomes a guiding light for young athletes, illustrating that their potential is boundless, not only in their chosen sport but in their ability to influence positive change, contribute to society, and cultivate a sense of purpose. Aspiring athletes are urged to embrace a balanced and fulfilling life that nurtures personal growth, community engagement, and a commitment to making a lasting impact on the world around them.

In the end, the hardwood may be where these icons made their mark, but it is merely a launchpad for a life lived with intention, passion, and a commitment to something greater than the game itself. The echoes of their success resonate far beyond the stadium, inspiring a generation to aim not just for the basket but for a slam dunk in the game of life.

In the world of basketball, certain players have transcended the court to become pioneers, breaking down societal barriers and reshaping the landscape of the game. These inspiring tales highlight the courage, resilience, and determination of individuals who shattered social, racial, or gender constraints, leaving an indelible mark on the sport.

The Racial Pioneer: Earl Lloyd

In the annals of basketball history, few stories resonate with as much significance and courage as that of Earl Lloyd, a trailblazer who shattered racial barriers and left an indelible mark on the sport. As the first African American to step onto an NBA court, Lloyd's journey transcends the confines of the basketball arena, embodying resilience, perseverance, and the relentless pursuit of equality.

Breaking Barriers in the Jim Crow Era

Earl Lloyd's story unfolded against the backdrop of the Jim Crow era, a time when racial segregation and discrimination were deeply entrenched in American society. Born in 1928, Lloyd grew up in segregated Virginia, where opportunities for black athletes were limited. Despite the odds stacked against him, his love for basketball and unwavering determination propelled him forward.

After a stellar collegiate career at West Virginia State University, Lloyd faced the daunting challenge of navigating racial prejudices as he aspired to play professionally. The racial climate of the time meant that opportunities for African American players were scarce, and the road to the NBA was fraught with obstacles.

The Historic Debut: October 31, 1950

On that fateful autumn night in 1950, Earl Lloyd etched his name in history as he took the court for the Washington Capitols, becoming the first black player to play in an NBA game. The significance of this moment went beyond the box score; it symbolized a seismic shift in the landscape of professional sports.

Lloyd faced overt racism both on and off the court. Taunts from opposing players and hostile crowds were part of the challenges he confronted. Yet, with a stoic demeanor and an unyielding commitment to the game, he persisted. His performance spoke volumes, transcending the color of his skin and demanding recognition for his skills and contributions.

Paving the Way for Generations to Come

Earl Lloyd's impact extended far beyond his playing days. His courage opened doors for future generations of black athletes, proving that talent and determination could triumph over prejudice. As the NBA gradually integrated, Lloyd's legacy became a beacon of inspiration for aspiring athletes who dared to dream despite societal constraints.

Lloyd's post-playing career was marked by his advocacy for equality and social justice. He became a mentor and role model, using his platform to champion civil rights causes and promote diversity in sports. His enduring commitment to breaking down racial barriers extended well into the fabric of the NBA, influencing policies and fostering an environment of inclusivity.

Conclusion: Earl Lloyd's Enduring Legacy

In "The Racial Pioneer: Earl Lloyd," we unravel the extraordinary journey of a man who defied the norms of his time, confronting racial prejudice with resilience and skill. Earl Lloyd's story is a testament to the transformative power of sports in challenging societal norms and fostering inclusivity. His legacy lives on, reminding us that the impact of breaking barriers extends far beyond the confines of the basketball court, shaping the narrative of equality for generations to come.

Queen of the Court: Lisa Leslie

In the annals of basketball history, certain names resonate as pioneers who transcended boundaries and shattered glass ceilings. Lisa Leslie stands as a living testament to resilience, skill, and an unyielding determination to redefine the narrative of women in basketball. In this chapter, we embark on a journey through the groundbreaking career of the Queen of the Court, Lisa Leslie.

Rise to Stardom: A Basketball Prodigy Emerges

Lisa Leslie's story begins on the blacktops of Inglewood, California, where her towering presence and unmatched skills quickly caught the attention of coaches and scouts. From high school phenom to college star at the University of Southern California, Leslie's journey was marked by an unwavering commitment to her craft. Her ability to dominate both ends of the court set her apart, foreshadowing the greatness that awaited her on a larger stage.

As Leslie's collegiate career soared, the anticipation surrounding her entry into the Women's National Basketball Association (WNBA) reached a fever pitch. In 1997, she was drafted by the Los Angeles Sparks, marking the beginning of a professional journey that would not only redefine her own legacy but also the perception of women in sports.

Challenges Faced: Breaking Through Barriers

The path to greatness is seldom smooth, and Lisa Leslie faced her share of challenges as a female athlete in a male-dominated arena. Battling stereotypes and skepticism, Leslie defied expectations with her skill, athleticism, and sheer determination. Her journey was a beacon for aspiring female basketball players, challenging the notion that the women's game was inferior or less entertaining than its male counterpart.

The chapter delves into the resilience Leslie displayed in the face of adversity, both on and off the court. From navigating gender biases to demanding equal recognition for women's basketball, she became an advocate for change, a voice that resonated far beyond the confines of the basketball court.

Impact on Redefining Perceptions: A Cultural Icon

As Lisa Leslie's star continued to rise, so did her impact on redefining perceptions of women in sports. She wasn't merely a basketball player; she became a cultural icon, breaking barriers and inspiring a generation of young girls to dream big. Leslie's influence reached beyond the court, challenging societal norms and encouraging a shift in the way female athletes were perceived and celebrated.

The chapter explores key moments in Leslie's career, from her multiple All-Star selections to her Olympic triumphs, showcasing how she became a symbol of empowerment for women worldwide. Through her grace, skill, and unapologetic confidence, Lisa Leslie not only left an indelible mark on the sport of basketball but also played a pivotal role in the ongoing journey towards gender equality in athletics.

In "Queen of the Court: Lisa Leslie," readers are invited to witness the remarkable journey of a trailblazer whose impact extends far beyond the confines of a basketball court, illustrating the transformative power of one individual's dedication to excellence and the courage to challenge the status quo.

The Asian Sensation: Jeremy Lin

In the annals of basketball history, certain stories transcend the court, resonating far beyond the bounds of the hardwood. The tale of Jeremy Lin, known as the "Linsanity" phenomenon, is one such narrative that captivated the world and shattered preconceived notions.

Breaking Stereotypes: The Early Years

Jeremy Lin's journey began in the basketball hotbeds of California, where he exhibited raw talent and an unyielding passion for the game. Despite his undeniable skills, Jeremy faced skepticism and prejudice due to his Asian heritage, a rarity in the NBA at the time. Coaches and scouts often overlooked him, blinded by stereotypes that dismissed the idea of an Asian player as a leading force in professional basketball.

Undeterred, Jeremy persisted. He navigated through college basketball, showcasing his prowess at Harvard, a platform that allowed him to demonstrate that talent knows no racial boundaries. His collegiate success, however, did little to sway the doubters who questioned whether he could replicate his achievements at the highest level of competition.

Linsanity Unleashed: Overcoming Cultural Barriers

The turning point came when Jeremy Lin, undrafted and seemingly overlooked, found a home with the New York Knicks. In the winter of 2012, Lin seized an opportunity thrust upon him due to injuries within the team. What followed was a meteoric rise, a phenomenon now etched in NBA lore as "Linsanity."

During this extraordinary period, Jeremy Lin not only dominated the court with his dazzling displays but also shattered cultural barriers. He became the first American player of Chinese or Taiwanese descent to find widespread success in the NBA. His performances weren't just a triumph for the Knicks; they were a triumph for every young aspiring basketball player who dared to dream, irrespective of their background.

Global Impact: Inspiring the Next Generation

The impact of Jeremy Lin's rise was felt far beyond the arenas of Madison Square Garden. Across continents, young athletes saw in him a beacon of hope and possibility. Jeremy Lin became a symbol of breaking through stereotypes, an inspiration for Asian-American youth who dared to pursue their dreams in a landscape dominated by a different narrative.

His jersey became a bestseller, not just in New York, but around the world. The underdog narrative, combined with his undeniable skill, resonated with fans who found a hero in the unassuming Asian-American point guard. It wasn't just about basketball anymore; it was about defying expectations, rewriting the script, and proving that talent and determination recognize no cultural or ethnic bounds.

Legacy Beyond the Court: Linsanity's Enduring Impact
As we explore the remarkable journey of Jeremy Lin, we delve into more than just a sports story. "The Asian Sensation" chapter underscores the power of representation, the courage to challenge stereotypes, and the transformative influence one individual can have on a global scale. Jeremy Lin's legacy is not confined to the games he played but extends to the countless aspiring players who found inspiration in his journey – a journey that transcends cultural barriers and reaffirms the universal language of basketball.

Beyond Borders: Manute Bol

In the realm of basketball, tales of extraordinary players often transcend the confines of the court. Manute Bol, a towering figure both in stature and impact, emerged not just as one of the tallest players in NBA history but as a beacon of hope, using his towering presence to advocate for social and humanitarian causes.

Rising from Sudan to the NBA

Manute Bol's journey began in Sudan, a place where dreams of NBA stardom seemed like distant echoes. Born into humble beginnings, Bol's exceptional height set him apart from an early age. As fate would have it, his raw talent captured the attention of scouts, leading to a remarkable journey from the war-torn landscapes of Sudan to the hardwood courts of the NBA.

Standing at 7 feet 7 inches, Bol's physical stature drew eyes, but it was his shot-blocking prowess and defensive skills that truly defined his legacy on the court. His time with the Washington Bullets and other NBA teams showcased not only his basketball prowess but also the resilience and determination that characterized his personal journey.

A Platform for Change

While Bol's impact on the court was undeniable, it was his off-court endeavors that truly set him apart. Recognizing the global spotlight that accompanied his NBA career, Bol chose to utilize his platform to shine a light on the issues plaguing his homeland. He became an outspoken advocate for peace and humanitarian causes in war-torn Sudan.

Bol's commitment extended beyond mere advocacy; he dedicated a significant portion of his earnings to support various charitable initiatives, providing aid and resources to those affected by the conflict in Sudan. Through his efforts, he exemplified the notion that athletes, regardless of their origin, possess the ability to effect positive change on a global scale.

Championing Education and Healthcare

Manute Bol's advocacy wasn't confined to geopolitical concerns alone. Recognizing the transformative power of education, he invested in projects that aimed to improve access to schooling and healthcare in Sudan. His vision went beyond the basketball court; it encompassed creating a legacy of positive change for future generations.

In this chapter, we unravel the remarkable journey of Manute Bol—beyond the statistics and game highlights. We explore how a Sudanese-born giant transcended the borders of basketball, using his influence to make a lasting impact on the world. Bol's story serves as a testament to the potential for athletes to become catalysts for change, reminding us that the impact of a player's legacy extends far beyond the boundaries of the game.

Breaking the Silence: Jason Collins

In the annals of basketball history, certain stories transcend the confines of the court, leaving an indelible mark on the sport and society at large. Jason Collins, a seasoned NBA veteran, etched his name into these pages as the first openly gay player in the NBA, breaking barriers and initiating a dialogue that resonated far beyond the hardwood.

Embracing Identity: The Courageous Revelation

For years, Jason Collins navigated the intricate dance between his passion for basketball and the fear of revealing his true self. The competitive and often unforgiving world of professional sports had been slow to embrace diversity, particularly regarding sexual orientation. In a groundbreaking moment, Jason chose authenticity over conformity, publicly acknowledging his identity as a gay man.

This revelation wasn't just a personal journey; it was a courageous stand against stereotypes and prejudice. The weight of being the first openly gay player in a major American professional sports league was immense, but Jason's decision was marked by a resilience that would inspire countless others facing similar struggles.

Impact on the League: Winds of Change

Jason Collins' disclosure sent ripples through the NBA and the broader sports community. The league, traditionally a bastion of athleticism and masculinity, faced a critical moment of introspection. The response was a mixture of support, skepticism, and curiosity. Yet, Jason's professionalism and dedication to his craft gradually dismantled misconceptions, proving that one's sexual orientation had no bearing on athletic prowess.

Teammates rallied around him, demonstrating that unity and acceptance could transcend preconceived notions. The NBA, in turn, embraced the opportunity to foster an environment of inclusivity, setting an example for other professional sports leagues.

Positive Change: A Catalyst for Inclusivity

Jason Collins became a catalyst for change, transforming the conversation around inclusivity in professional sports. His journey sparked discussions not only within the NBA but across various sports platforms, challenging stereotypes and fostering a more accepting culture. The impact reached beyond the locker room, influencing fans, aspiring athletes, and advocates for equality.

As the NBA welcomed diversity, it signaled a broader societal shift toward recognizing and celebrating differences. Jason Collins' story not only paved the way for LGBTQ+ athletes but also prompted organizations to reevaluate their commitment to inclusivity, laying the foundation for a more diverse and welcoming future in professional sports.

In "Breaking the Silence: Jason Collins," we explore the bravery, resilience, and positive impact of an athlete who transcended the game, leaving an enduring legacy that echoes the importance of authenticity, acceptance, and breaking barriers in the pursuit of a more inclusive world.

The Dream Team: The 1992 USA Women's Basketball

In the annals of basketball history, the year 1992 is synonymous with the iconic "Dream Team" that dominated the men's basketball scene at the Barcelona

Olympics. However, amidst the hoopla surrounding the men's success, there emerged another force that was rewriting the narrative of women's basketball—the 1992 USA Women's Basketball team.

This formidable squad, composed of some of the most talented and trailblazing female athletes, embarked on a journey that transcended the boundaries of sport. At a time when women's basketball was often relegated to the shadows, the 1992 USA Women's team stepped onto the global stage with an unwavering determination to challenge gender norms and elevate the status of women's basketball.

Breaking Barriers: Challenging Gender Norms

The 1992 USA Women's Basketball team shattered stereotypes with their unparalleled skill, agility, and sheer determination. Coached by a visionary leader who believed in the untapped potential of women in sports, this team showcased a brand of basketball that was just as thrilling and skillful as its male counterpart. Their performance on the court sent a powerful message that women could excel at the highest levels of the game.

In an era when women's sports were often undervalued, the Dream Team became a symbol of empowerment. The players, with their dazzling displays of athleticism, proved that the court was not a domain reserved exclusively for men. They challenged preconceived notions about the capabilities of female athletes and demonstrated that women could command the same respect and admiration as their male counterparts.

Paving the Way for Growth: The Legacy Continues

The impact of the 1992 USA Women's Basketball team extended far beyond the Olympic arena. Their success ignited a spark that fueled the growth of women's basketball globally. Young girls who aspired to dribble, shoot, and score saw role models in these athletes, realizing that their dreams were not bound by gender constraints.

The Dream Team laid the foundation for the evolution of women's basketball, inspiring generations of players to come. The increased visibility and recognition garnered by female athletes in the aftermath of the 1992 Olympics played a pivotal role in dismantling barriers and fostering a more inclusive and equitable environment for women in sports.

As we reflect on the achievements of the 1992 USA Women's Basketball team, we celebrate not only their prowess on the court but also their enduring legacy in challenging gender norms and paving the way for the continued growth and recognition of women's basketball on the global stage. Their story is a testament to the transformative power of sports in reshaping societal perceptions and creating opportunities for athletes, regardless of gender, to shine brightly on the world stage.

From the Street to the Court: Stephon Marbury

In the bustling streets of Coney Island, New York, where challenges and hardships were as common as the sounds of the city, a young boy named Stephon Marbury discovered his love for basketball. Raised in a neighborhood that often presented tough choices, Marbury found solace and purpose on the local courts. Little did he know that this humble beginning would pave the way for an extraordinary journey that transcended borders and cultures.

A Rising Star on the New York Courts
Marbury's talent was undeniable from an early age. As a high school prodigy, he mesmerized crowds with his lightning-quick crossovers and precise three-pointers. The basketball courts of New York City served as both his proving ground and his sanctuary, offering an escape from the challenges of his surroundings.

His journey through high school and college showcased not only his athletic prowess but also his resilience in the face of adversity. As he rose through the ranks, the young point guard earned accolades and attention, capturing the imagination of basketball enthusiasts beyond the city limits.

The NBA Stage: Trials and Triumphs

Entering the NBA draft with high expectations, Marbury faced the pressures of professional basketball. His journey through various teams in the league, from the Minnesota Timberwolves to the New Jersey Nets and beyond, was marked by dazzling plays and personal challenges. Yet, it was his time with the Phoenix Suns where Marbury truly showcased his skills, earning All-Star nods and leaving an indelible mark on the league.

However, as with any narrative of triumph, Marbury's story also bore the weight of setbacks. The NBA, with its demanding schedule and rigorous expectations, took a toll on the talented point guard. Despite the trials, Marbury's resilience shone through, and his journey took an unexpected turn that would forever change the course of his career and legacy.

A New Chapter Unfolds in China

The next chapter in Stephon Marbury's life saw him embarking on a unique and groundbreaking adventure in China. Embracing a new culture and language, Marbury joined the Chinese Basketball Association (CBA), becoming a member of the Beijing Ducks. Little did he know that this move would transform him from a basketball star to a cultural icon.

As he adapted to the intricacies of Chinese basketball, Marbury also became a cultural bridge, connecting people through the universal language of the sport. His impact went beyond the court; it resonated with a nation that embraced him not just as an athlete but as a symbol of resilience, determination, and the boundless possibilities of sports diplomacy.

Bridging Cultural Gaps: Marbury's Enduring Legacy
This segment explores how Stephon Marbury's journey from the streets of Coney Island to the courts of China became a powerful narrative of cultural exchange. Through his experiences, challenges, and triumphs, Marbury demonstrated the unifying power of basketball, proving that the love for the game could transcend

geographical and cultural boundaries. His story serves as a testament to the transformative nature of sports, showing that sometimes, a bouncing ball can bring people together in ways that surpass the confines of language and tradition.

The International Ambassador: Yao Ming

In the vast tapestry of basketball's global reach, one towering figure stands out not just for his prowess on the court but for the diplomatic role he inadvertently assumed. Yao Ming, a towering center from China, not only ascended to stardom in the NBA but also emerged as a cultural ambassador, weaving threads of understanding between Eastern and Western worlds.

Yao Ming's journey began in the heart of Shanghai, where his exceptional height and burgeoning skills caught the attention of basketball scouts. His dream of playing in the NBA seemed like a distant fantasy, considering the geographical and cultural barriers that separated the East from the West. However, Yao's indomitable spirit and unwavering dedication propelled him to overcome these challenges.

In 2002, when Yao Ming was selected as the first overall pick by the Houston Rockets, he became a symbol of hope for aspiring Chinese basketball players and a trailblazer for international athletes seeking success in the NBA. His impact was immediate, not just in the stat sheets, but in the hearts and minds of millions who tuned in to witness a new chapter in basketball history.

Beyond the confines of the court, Yao Ming assumed an unexpected role as a cultural bridge. As he navigated the challenges of adapting to a new country and a different style of play, he simultaneously opened a window for Western audiences to gain insights into Chinese culture. His humility, work ethic, and genuine personality made him a beloved figure on both sides of the Pacific.

Yao Ming's influence transcended the confines of the basketball arena. Recognizing the potential of sports as a tool for cultural exchange, he actively engaged in initiatives that promoted understanding between East and West. His involvement in charity work, cultural exchange programs, and his tireless efforts to bridge the gap between two vastly different worlds showcased his commitment to fostering global unity through the universal language of basketball.

The impact of Yao Ming's journey reverberates not only in the accolades he earned on the court but in the countless young athletes who dared to dream beyond borders. His legacy extends far beyond the three-point line, leaving an indelible mark on the interconnectedness of cultures through the transformative power of sports. Yao Ming stands as a testament to the notion that basketball, at its core, is a medium for building bridges and fostering understanding among diverse communities across the globe.

Conclusion: Empowering Dreams Beyond the Court
In the rich tapestry of basketball narratives, the tales of resilience and triumph over adversity serve as a compelling reminder that the game transcends the boundaries of the court. As we reflect on the inspiring journeys of these athletes, we witness the transformative power of basketball not merely as a sport but as a catalyst for change, unity, and boundless dreams.

The stories contained within these pages are not just about victories on the scoreboard; they are about the victories of the human spirit. They illuminate how, in the face of daunting challenges, the passion for basketball becomes a guiding light, a force that propels individuals to overcome adversity and redefine their own limitations. The hardwood becomes a canvas where dreams are painted with the sweat and determination of those who refuse to be defined by their circumstances.

Basketball, as a powerful force for change, emerges as a unifying thread that weaves through diverse backgrounds, cultures, and life experiences. It is a language spoken by people of all ages, races, and nationalities, fostering connections that go beyond the confines of the game itself. These stories stand as testaments to the idea that a shared love for basketball can bridge gaps, dismantle barriers, and create a global community bound by a common passion.

As we witness the resilience of players who have faced adversity head-on, we are reminded that basketball is not merely a game of physical prowess; it is a canvas for the human spirit to paint tales of triumph. The court becomes a stage where personal narratives unfold, showcasing the resilience, perseverance, and indomitable will of those who dare to dream.

These stories compel us to look beyond traditional limitations, encouraging the next generation of players to envision possibilities that stretch beyond the boundaries of convention. Through the pages of this collection, we invite young readers to embrace the transformative power of basketball, allowing it to be a source of inspiration, empowerment, and a reminder that dreams, no matter how audacious, are within reach.

In the echoes of these narratives, we find a collective call to action—a call to nurture the dreams of aspiring athletes, to champion inclusivity, and to celebrate the universal language of basketball that unites us all. As the final buzzer sounds on these stories, it signals not an end but a beginning—an invitation to continue the journey, to dream boldly, and to let the enduring spirit of basketball be a beacon that guides us all toward a future defined by passion, perseverance, and the pursuit of our highest aspirations.

In the pulsating world of basketball, where the spotlight often shines on dazzling slam dunks and buzzer-beaters, it is the unsung heroes on the sidelines that wield an unparalleled influence. Coaches, with their wisdom, guidance, and mentorship, don the responsibility of not just crafting skilled players but molding responsible individuals who carry the spirit of the game beyond the court.

The Mentorship of Coach Johnson: A Legacy Beyond the Court

In the quaint embrace of a small town, Coach Johnson's impact echoed far beyond the hardwood courts where the squeak of sneakers and the rhythm of bouncing basketballs resonated. His coaching legacy transcended the confines of wins and losses, becoming a guiding light for players who sought not just athletic prowess but a compass for life's journey.

Coach Johnson's coaching strategies were indeed impeccable, his playbook a testament to years of experience and basketball acumen. Yet, it was his unwavering commitment to character development that etched his name into the collective memory of the community. His players, a tapestry of diverse talents and backgrounds, would later recount their time under his tutelage not solely in terms of victories but as a transformative journey of self-discovery.

In Coach Johnson's world, basketball was more than a game—it was a classroom for life's essential lessons. Through countless practices and games, he wove a narrative of perseverance, teamwork, and integrity into the very fabric of his coaching philosophy. Players emerged not only with refined skills but with a profound understanding that success was not solely measured by the numbers on a scoreboard.

One poignant illustration of Coach Johnson's impact unfolded in the life of a star player grappling with off-court tribulations. In a moment when many would have focused solely on statistics and performance, Coach Johnson demonstrated a rare depth of compassion. He became a pillar of support, extending understanding and encouragement when it was needed most. The coach saw beyond the jersey, recognizing the individual behind the player and understanding that life's challenges often seep onto the court.

It was in these moments of mentorship that Coach Johnson's coaching transcended the transactional nature of sports. He became not just a coach but a confidant, a mentor who shaped destinies with the same precision he used to draw up game-winning plays. The player, once burdened with personal struggles, found solace and guidance in the coach's steadfast support. It was a testament to the belief that the impact of a coach goes beyond the court, reaching into the intricate tapestry of a player's life.

As the sun set on Coach Johnson's coaching career, his legacy lingered, not just in championship banners and trophy cases, but in the character of the individuals he nurtured. His small town, once a backdrop to a basketball court, now stood as a testament to the enduring influence of a mentor who understood that the game of basketball was, above all, a platform for shaping lives and building futures. Coach Johnson's legacy lived on, a testament to the transformative power of mentorship that transcends the boundaries of sports and enriches the human spirit.

Beyond the Scoreboard: Lessons Beyond Wins and Losses

In the world of competitive sports, wins and losses often overshadow the journey of personal growth. Coach Ramirez, a veteran in the coaching arena, made it his mission to emphasize that success isn't solely measured by the scoreboard. His team's journey was marked by character-building moments: acknowledging opponents, handling defeat with grace, and celebrating victories with humility.

Through a series of team-building exercises and community service initiatives, Coach Ramirez transformed his players into ambassadors of goodwill. Their impact extended beyond the court as they became role models for younger athletes, demonstrating that true success is measured by the positive influence one has on others.

Developing Leaders: The Legacy of Coach Parker

Coach Parker's impact extended far beyond the confines of the basketball court, reaching into the very fabric of his players' lives and the communities they touched. His unique coaching philosophy was not merely about drawing up plays or securing victories; it was a transformative approach aimed at cultivating leaders who would make a lasting difference both in the sporting arena and society at large.

In recognizing and harnessing the leadership potential within each player, Coach Parker set the stage for a ripple effect of positive change. His commitment went beyond the scoreboard; it delved into the personal growth of every individual under his guidance. By empowering players to take charge, communicate effectively, and inspire their teammates, Coach Parker was sculpting a generation of young leaders.

The success of Coach Parker's approach manifested not only in the wins and championships but also in the way his players emerged as pillars of their communities. As these young individuals stepped into leadership roles, they carried with them the values instilled by their coach—values of integrity, accountability, and the importance of collaboration. The basketball court served as their training ground, shaping them into resilient, empathetic leaders capable of navigating the challenges that awaited them beyond the game.

The legacy of Coach Parker is evident in the stories of his former players who, armed with the lessons learned on the court, went on to become influential figures in their communities. Whether leading youth programs, spearheading charitable initiatives, or advocating for positive change, these individuals became living testaments to the profound impact of mentorship that goes beyond the game of basketball.

Coach Parker's coaching philosophy, centered on developing leaders, serves as a timeless reminder that sports have the potential to be a powerful catalyst for positive societal change. His legacy lives on not just in the accolades his players achieved but in the enduring impact they continue to make as leaders, mentors, and champions of the values instilled by a coach who saw beyond the court—an impact that echoes through the generations and leaves an indelible mark on the very fabric of our communities.

Conclusion: The Everlasting Impact of Coaching for Character

As we conclude this chapter, we have traversed through real-life narratives that illuminate the profound influence coaches wield beyond the tactical intricacies of the game. What emerges is a testament to the transformative power of mentors who, with a keen understanding, transcend the Xs and Os to shape individuals who embody the very essence of basketball's spirit.

The stories shared here serve as a vivid reminder that the basketball court is more than just a battleground for athletic prowess; it is a microcosm of life itself. Coaches, often unsung heroes on the sidelines, recognize that the skills honed and the values instilled in players during their formative years on the court extend far beyond the hardwood floors. These mentors understand that the lessons learned in practice sessions and under the glare of stadium lights are invaluable building blocks for the character and resilience needed in the broader arena of life.

"Coaching for Character" goes beyond the wins and losses, shining a spotlight on the pivotal role mentors play in shaping not just basketball players, but well-rounded individuals. The coach becomes a guide, imparting not only strategic acumen but life skills that instill responsibility, perseverance, and integrity. In this realm, the basketball court serves as a canvas for character development, where every bounce of the ball becomes a metaphor for overcoming obstacles, and every huddle an opportunity for instilling the values that will endure long after the final buzzer.

As we celebrate the achievements of players who've risen to greatness under the guidance of these coaches, we also acknowledge the enduring legacy these mentors leave. The impact isn't confined to championships or highlight reels; it lives on in the ethical decisions players make, the leadership roles they assume, and the positive influence they wield in their communities. "Coaching for Character" illuminates the profound understanding that, beyond the athletic arena, coaches are architects of character, sculptors of resilience, and mentors who shape individuals poised to make meaningful contributions to society.

In the broader arena of life, where challenges are diverse and victories come in myriad forms, the essence of basketball, as instilled by these coaches, serves as a beacon. It propels individuals toward becoming responsible, resilient leaders, carrying with them the indomitable spirit of the game—a spirit that transcends boundaries, leaving an enduring impact on the collective human experience.